THE AMERICAN DREAM
IN AFRICAN AMERICAN, ASIAN AMERICAN,
AND HISPANIC AMERICAN DRAMA

August Wilson, Frank Chin, and Luis Valdez

THE AMERICAN DREAM
IN AFRICAN AMERICAN, ASIAN AMERICAN, AND HISPANIC AMERICAN DRAMA

August Wilson, Frank Chin, and Luis Valdez

Tsui-fen Jiang

With a Foreword by
Yu-cheng Lee

The Edwin Mellen Press
Lewiston•Queenston•Lampeter

Library of Congress Cataloging-in-Publication Data

Jiang, Tsui-fen.
The American dream in African American, Asian American, and Hispanic American
drama : August Wilson, Frank Chin, and Luis Valdez / Tsui-fen Jiang ; with a foreword
by Yu-cheng Lee.
    p. cm.
Includes bibliographical references and index.
ISB N-13: 978-0-7734-4656-4
ISBN-10: 0-7734-4656-7
I. Title.

hors série.

A CIP catalog record for this book is available from the British Library.

Front cover: Photo from the Salina Community Theatre, Inc. production of August Wilson's
The Piano, October 2004, with the permission of Samuel French licensing. Photo credit given
to J. R. Lidgett.

The Edwin Mellen Press
Box 450
Lewiston, New York
USA 14092-0450

The Edwin Mellen Press
Box 67
Queenston, Ontario
CANADA L0S 1L0

The Edwin Mellen Press, Ltd.
Lampeter, Ceredigion, Wales
UNITED KINGDOM SA48 8LT

Printed in the United States of America

To my parents

Table of Contents

Foreword

Tsui-fen Jiang's *The American Dream in African American, Asian American, and Hispanic American Drama* is a timely book. It arrives at a time when new life is being breathed into the American dream as a result of Obama's election, and American society is again enthused by the spirit of optimism despite the enormity of the challenges the nation faces, specifically "two wars, a planet in peril, [and] the worse financial crisis in a century," in the new president's own words. It is therefore most significant that Jiang calls our attention to the stark reality confronting American ethnic playwrights—a reality in which many members of ethnic minorities are deprived of economic opportunities and social justice. For these ethnic playwrights, the American dream sometimes assumes a nightmarish aspect.

The plays under discussion here include August Wilson's *The Piano Lesson*, Frank Chin's *The Chickencoop Chinaman*, and Luis Valdez's *Zoot Suit*, all canonical works in the tradition of American minority drama. By employing various modern theories to make sense of these plays, Jiang's study shows, in an intelligent manner, how literature and politics together disclose the limits of the American dream. For Jiang, these plays are to be read as national allegories because they represent general historical experiences of American minority peoples. They are projects which try to claim, in Jiang's words, "the minority people's American dream of three tenets—to rectify their internalized distorted self-image, to implant self-esteem, and to earn their due respect from whites and others." Apart from these tenets, the plays also share a common feature: they call for a "coalition or solidarity" within and among minority groups to struggle against social-economical exploitation and racial discrimination. In other words, these are works to be recognized as strongly inclined to engage in what Edward W. Said calls "worldliness." They not only bring into question the idea of the American dream, but also offer alternative versions of that dream, which involve what Jiang refers to as "the reconstruction of a healthy ethnic subjectivity."

This is a finely written book. Tsui-fen Jiang is confident in her deployment of theoretical acumen and critical analysis, and makes an obviously important contribution to the scholarship on both the American dream and American ethnic literature.

Yu-cheng Lee
Academia Sinica, Taiwan

Yu-cheng Lee completed his doctorate in comparative literature at National Taiwan University in 1986. He is currently Distinguished Research Fellow and Director at the Institute of European and American Studies, Academia Sinica, Taiwan. He also holds a joint-appointment as Professor of Literature at National Sun Yat-sen University. His recent publications include *In the Age of Theory* (2006), *Transgression: Towards a Critical Study of African American Literature and Culture* (2007) and *Before the Statue of Gandhi and Other London Essays* (2008), all published in Taipei by Asian Culture.

Acknowledgements

I would like to thank my friends and colleagues, Tzu-chung Su, Wei-jan Chi, Yu-cheng Lee, Hsin-ling Wang, Erick Heroux, Ruth Martin and Huang-yi Hsia, for generously sharing their expertise and their friendship with me throughout this project. I would like to particularly thank my assistant Jessica Pei-jung Shao for her kind and patient assistance in making this book possible. Financial support for this project included National Science Council and National Chengchi University in Taiwan. Finally, I thank my parents, my husband Kuo-kang, my daughter Ning, and my son Kuan. I could not have written this book without your love and support.

Chapter One
Introduction

The American dream has been an important theme in American literature. One principal reason for such a phenomenon can be attributed to the representative spirit of the nation, and the equal opportunity for everyone and anyone to pursue their ideals, or dreams. America has always been the promised land for diverse peoples to realize their dreams. Eric Sevareid in his article "The American Dream" published in 1970 puts the representative spirit succinctly in one word—freedom (4). For early white immigrants in search of religious freedom, for later Asians or Mexicans in search of better material provision, America is their dream country. Former US President Bill Clinton in his speech to the Democratic Leadership Council in 1993 states,

> The American dream that we were all raised on is a simple but powerful one—if you work hard and play by the rules you should be given a chance to go as far as your God-given ability will take you. (qtd. in Hochschild, 18)

This country has also presented itself as a "promised land" even though for the past two hundred years it has barred many people from a chance to realize their dreams. Accordingly, American literature has faithfully depicted how these peoples have pursued their American dreams.

As scholar Jennifer L. Hochschild states in her major book *Facing up to the American Dream: Race, Class, and the Soul of the Nation* published in 1995, "The American dream is deeply embedded in most American's images of themselves and their society" (259). The concept of the American dream is ingrained in Americans, be they whites or minorities. However, the significance of the American dream to the ethnic groups might be different from that of whites, and the attainability of the American dream might be even tougher for these ethnic groups. In this book, I chose three plays for the research to explore how ethnic playwrights manifest the difficulties for non-whites to realize their American dream. In chronological order, they are Frank Chin's *The Chickencoop Chinaman* (1972), Luis Valdez's *Zoot Suit* (1978), and August Wilson's *The Piano Lesson* (1987), representing respectively dramas of the three major ethnic groups in America—Asian American, Hispanic American, and African American.

I. The American Dream for White Americans

The concept of the American dream might differ from person to person; however, a myriad of academic scholars, popular writers, politicians, and street poets have argued that one of the most pervasive myths in the United States is this so-called "American dream." After a review of the literature from a diversity of disciplines such as sociology, philosophy, anthropology, communication and folklore, scholar Alan D. DeSantis divides over thirty individual concepts that make up the conception of "the American dream" into eight distinct themes. These eight themes are the "stuff this dream is made of:"

> 1) Freedom: The promise that one can live without the threat of arbitrary physical or mental abuse.
> 2) Equality: The promise that one will have equal access to all rights and privileges.
> 3) Democracy: The promise that one can determine one's own political and social state through elections.
> 4) Religious Independence: The promise that one can determine one's

own religious affiliation.
5) Wealth: The promise that one can procure money, property, and the good life that accompanies such acquisitions.
6) Puritan Work Ethic: The promise that one is able to find meaningful work.
7) New Beginnings: The promise that one can start anew.
8) Consumption and Leisure: The promise that one can secure products and services that aid a lifestyle marked by realization and self-indulgence. (480)

As inclusive as it can be, DeSantis's list of the eight themes connotes that with effort, hard work, optimism, and equality, anyone in America can achieve material success and enjoy the freedom, leisure, and religious and social independence that attend wealthy economic status. However, under these eight themes lies a paradox of materialistic and spiritualistic aspirations. When analyzing these two apparently dichotomous longings, Walter Fisher argues that this American dream myth consists of "two dreams, or more accurately, it is two myths, myths that we all share in some degree or the other and which, when taken together, characterize America as a culture" (160). Similarly, James R. Andrew regards one of the most persistent strains to which Americans have been subjected is "that of dealing with the demands placed on them by professed moral imperatives while, at the same time, experiencing the strong urge to succeed" (316). The American dream thus is constituted by material success (wealth and comfort) and spiritual values (equality and tolerance).

While the conception of the American dream is involved with material and moral longings, most ordinary people naturally associate it with a self-made hero who has economic and material success. Warren Buffet, Bill Clinton, Bill Gates are just a few examples of success story representatives. Nowadays, more examples can be found among such show business and sports stars as Oprah Winfrey, Tiger Woods, and Kobe Bryant. This is why some scholars argue,

"While there are a variety of components to this dream, none competes with the promise of economic and material success" (Cernkovich et al. 131). It is easy to understand that possessing sovereignty over the White House or multibillion assets garners the recognition of fulfilling one's American dream.

It is difficult for one living in America not to be bombarded by images of materialism and economic achievement. However, the pervasive impact of such a notion of the American dream also incurs both positive and negative consequences. While the power of the American dream has inspired people to strive for success, it has also frustrated a great number of citizens of that country. "The dream has inspired heroic individual success stories, but it also has expressed itself in nightmares and human misery" (Cernkovich et al. 131).

In literature, there are faithful renditions of the pursuit of the American dream. For example, F. Scott Fitzgerald in *The Great Gatsby* (1925) depicts the negative consequences of pursuing the American dream at the mercy of moral imperatives. What was originally about discovery, individualism, and the pursuit of happiness is replaced by corruption, dishonesty, and mere pursuit of wealth.

In his book entitled *Family, Drama, and American Dreams*, Tom Scanlan, however, finds that "American drama in the twentieth century has been strikingly preoccupied with problems of family life" (4). Based on his extensive research on American drama, Scanlan in this book, published in 1978, regarded the dreams of Americans closely connected to the "concern of family failure and destruction" (7). The concern of family and the American dream best merge in Arthur Miller's *Death of a Salesman* (1949), which also examines the cost of blind faith in the American dream. William Heyen in his "Arthur Miller's *Death of a Salesman* and the American Dream" points out that the protagonist, Willy Loman, has "a dream of being respected and successful and loved" (53). Dazzled by the booming post-war economy, Willy not only believes in the material drive of the American dream but also instructs his sons to continue working for this capitalist materialism. To be more precise, the American dream in *Death of the Salesman* culminates in Willy's projected goal of top salesman—a rich and well-liked man. Even until his death, he never realizes that the personal truth and moral vision of the American dream are the insights he needs. In the Requiem, the epilogue of the play, his two sons announce the impact of Willy's American dream; while Biff asserts that Willy had "the wrong dreams" (953), Happy thinks his father's dream is good. With the determination to win it for Willy, he affirms, "It's the only dream you can have—to come out number-one man" (954). The playwright, at the end of the play, seems to have reinforced the material allure of the American dream through the vision of the younger Loman.

It is obvious that American writers are more preoccupied with the American nightmare than the American dream. However, the idea of the American dream keeps emitting its charm to motivate people to reach their goal. Examining over one hundred novels written after 1960, Kathryn Hume finds the dichotomous appeals of the American dream salient in American fiction. In her *American Dream American Nightmare*, the American dream is epitomized in three simple promises—equality, justice, and prosperity (10). She agrees that among the three, material success is the principal attraction. "Prosperity for anyone willing to work hard is a crucial component of the Dream, a house of one's own being the icon" (Hume 3). In addition to prosperity, the American dream also entails a moral or spiritual vision which guarantees some certain liberties in America: "freedom of worship, justice in the courts, and a classless society (or at least one where the class barriers were permeable to those who educated themselves)" (Hume 3).

II. The American Dream for Non-Whites: Its Unique Significance and the

Indispensable Way to Its Fulfillment

Viewed from the spiritual perspective, the American dream refers to the ideal embodiment of freedom and equality; viewed from the material perspective, it means the ultimate realization of fame and wealth. The dichotomous appeals are revealed on whites' and non-whites' aspirations respectively. For whites whose civil rights are safeguarded by the Constitution, "the most common understanding of the American dream" is "achieving economic success" (Hochschild 93). While their white counterparts tend to strive more for the material aspect of the American dream, the ethnic groups aim more at achieving the spiritual American dream before fulfilling the material one. While collecting materials for the American dream in literature or drama, I discovered that (white) scholars in the 1970s primarily examine the material aspect of the American dream. For example, the aforementioned article entitled "The American Dream" by Severeid stresses that people are free to pursue more riches, whereas the book *Family, Drama, American Dreams* by Scanlan presents the family strife in Eugene O'Neill's, Arthur Miller's, and Tennessee Williams's plays. These scholars in the 1970s probably did not expect that since that decade a plethora of American ethnic playwrights would have placed their emphasis on a different kind of American dream. The characters in these ethnic writings certainly wish to fulfill their material American dream; however, it seems before they can feel free to pursue their economic success, they are impelled to confront the more imminent issue of the spiritual aspect of the American dream.

The divergence between whites' and non-whites' recognitions of the American dream lies in the radically different experiences and treatments they have received in this dream country. It was white immigrants who conquered and founded America, and settled this new country. They have been the majority who made the laws, and who prescribed rights for the citizens. Therefore, freedom and equality have been given to whites. But African Americans, Asian Americans, Hispanic Americans, and other ethnicities have a more profound understanding of the American dream. The majority of these minorities have heart-rending and traumatic histories of when they settled in this country. Although African Americans did not come of their own free will, having lived in this country for over four centuries, they have also taken the idea of the American dream as part of their culture. They have had a difficult time adjusting themselves to America, a land dominated by whites who have exploited and discriminated against them. Likewise, other ethnic groups have gone through the same pattern. Owing to their racial memories of pain and denigration, they know the American dream signifies something more than economic success to them.

As Bruce Springsteen puts it, "I don't think the American dream was that everybody was going to make... a billion dollars, but it was that everybody was going to have an opportunity and the chance to live a life with some decency and some dignity and a chance for some self-respect" (qtd. in Hochschild 264). This remark implies that non-whites were not given a fair chance to lead a life of decency, dignity, and self-respect. It then is no wonder that major ethnic dramatists are all preoccupied with why their own people cannot live with dignity, decency and self-respect. This has a lot to do with their wounded subjectivity as a consequence of their distorted past and history. Accordingly, in American ethnic drama, the American dream is tantamount to the reconstruction of a healthy ethnic subjectivity. In other words, American ethnic drama unanimously projects the minority people's American dream of three tenets—to rectify their internalized distorted self-image, to implant self-esteem, and to earn their due respect from whites and others. In addition to these three common tenets, the three plays sampled for discussion in this book also share one striking feature: coalition or solidarity within their ethnic group, other minority groups, or even friendly majority group members.

III. Literature Review and the New Look

Many scholars have paid attention to this particular myth of the American dream. For example, books such as Jennifer L. Hochschild's *Facing up to the American Dream: Race, Class, and the Soul of the Nation* (1995) and Robert Johnson's *The American Dream* (2000), and articles such as Walter R. Fisher's "Reaffirmation and Subversion of the American Dream" (1973), and Alan D. DeSantis's "Selling the American Dream Myth to Black Southerners: The Chicago Defender and the Great Migration of 1915-1919" (1998). The scholars of the 1970s and before tended to read the significance and development of the American dream from a white point of view. Recent studies, however, have found race an important factor in the different understandings of this American myth. The aforementioned book by Hochschild thus highlights the difficulties for blacks to pursue material success.

When the American dream is depicted in literature, scholars detect a paradox under this powerful dream in multicultural American society. For example, books such as *American Dreams, American Nightmares* (1970) edited by David Madden, *The Frontier Experience and the American Dream* (1989) edited by David Mogen, Mark Busby, and Paul Bryant, and *American Dream, American Nightmare: Fiction Since 1960* (2002) written by Kathryn Hume all examine the impact of the dichotomous attractions of the American dream. Except for the very brief mention of the Indians and blacks in the introduction (xxiii, xxxi-xxxii, xxxix) and one article devoted to Ralph Ellison's *Invisible Man*, the nineteen articles of *American Dreams, American Nightmares* principally focus on white writers' concepts and their works of the American dreams and nightmares. With an emphasis on the white perspective on the American dream, most of the eighteen papers collected in *The Frontier Experience and the American Dream* discuss the frontier spirit or myth as a major component of the American dream. However, as published in the late 1980s, the book incorporates the multicultural perspective and includes one paper on American Indian literature and two on Chicano literature, both with a focus on fiction. Hume's *American Dream, American Nightmare: Fiction Since 1960*, a book which has inspired me greatly, however, differs from the previous works in its new concern with race. After scrutinizing one hundred novels of the past four decades, Hume asserts that the notion of the American dream has misled new immigrants and minorities in America.

Much neglected by the aforementioned scholars is American drama. Furthermore, American ethnic drama of the 1970s and after is an exciting arena with many ethnic playwrights voicing themselves with regard to their view of the American dream. Each of the three plays to be discussed in this book as the representatives of the three ethnic dramas respectively has initiated much academic interest. In the case of Wilson's *The Piano Lesson,* Kim Pereira's *August Wilson and the African-American Odyssey* (1995), Sandra Shannon's *The Dramatic Vision of August Wilson* (1995), Peter Wolfe's *August Wilson* (1999), *May All Your Fences Have Gates: Essays on the Drama of August Wilson* (1994) edited by Alan Nadel, *August Wilson: A Casebook* (2000) edited by Marilyn Elkins all have important analyses of this play. Most important of all, Harry J. Elam Jr.'s seminal book *The Past as Present in the Drama of August Wilson* (2004) is full of insightful discussion on Wilson's works. There are also numerous articles devoted to the reading of *The Piano Lesson*. But hardly any of them has connected the play with the issue of blacks' American dream.

Likewise, quite a few scholars have explored the problem depicted in Chin's *The Chickencoop Chinaman*, but there is no one single book devoted to Chin's drama or Chinese/Asian American drama. Several important Taiwanese scholars have drawn special attention to Chin's writing due to his prominent militant promulgation of "masculine writing"[1] in f literature. Yu-cheng Lee's "The Politics of Remembering in Donald Duk" (1994), Te-hsing Shan and Wen-ching Ho's *Cultural Identity and Chinese American Literature* (1994), and Te-hsing Shan's *Inscriptions and Representations: Chinese American Literary and Cultural Studies* (2000) all touch upon the same issue of Chin's preoccupation with masculinity. Many prestigious scholars in America have also discussed a similar controversy in their journal papers and book chapters, but very few of them are devoted to the reading of the American dream in this play. For example, King-Kok Cheung's "The Woman Warrior versus the Chinaman Pacific: Must a Chinese American Critic Choose between Feminism and Heroism?" (1990), Shirley Geok-lin Lim's "Growing with Stories': Chinese American Identities, Textual Identities"(1996) and "The Ambivalent American: Asian American Literature on the Cusp"(1992), and David Leiwei Li's *Imagining the Nation* (1998) deal with Chin's representation of Chinese American subjectivity and identity, but they rarely focus on the way to the American dream for Chinese America in Chin's plays. The most important and most recent work related to the study of Chin's play is Daniel Y. Kim's *Writing Manhood in Black and Yellow: Ralph Ellison, Frank Chin, and the Literary Politics of Identity* (2005), a book with a lengthy discussion on Chin's plays. However, different from Kim's

---

[1] In order to deconstruct the white stereotypical impression of Asian men, Chin is keen on evoking the masculine and heroic features of Chinese man in his writing. When constructing a Chinese "heroic tradition, he emphasizes "masculine writing"—"martial heroism and a masculine code of honor" (Chu 118).

negative view of Chin's *The Chickencoop Chinaman*, I shall offer an optimistic reading of the play with regard to the notion of the American dream.

Compared with the studies on Wilson's and Chin's plays, there are not that many books and papers on Valdez's *Zoot Suit*. Carl R. Shirley and Paula W. Shirley in *Understanding Chicano Literature* (1988) particularly praise this play and have an inspiring discussion on this play. Dramatist and scholar Jorge A. Huerta in his *Chicano Theater: Themes and Forms* (1982) also draws our attention to the issue of ethnicity and identity in *Zoot Suit*. Harry J. Elam Jr.'s *Taking It to the Streets: The Social Protest Theater of Luis Valdez and Amiri Baraka* (1997) offers a detailed analysis on Valdez's resistance strategy and achievement. Moreover, both Carole Hamilton in *Drama for Students* (1999) and Elizabeth Ramirez in "Chicano Theatre Reaches the Professional Stage: Luis Valdez's *Zoot Suit*" (1996) focus on the Chicano feature in the play. But again, they do not approach the play from the perspective of the American dream. Nor do they pay a lot of attention to the positive significance of the non-Hispanic characters in the play.

Although there is plenty of research on *The Piano Lesson*, *The Chickencoop Chinaman*, and *Zoot Suit*, none has placed the focus on the specific American dream embedded in the texts. Moreover, none has attempted to treat the plays and/or three ethnic dramas simultaneously. The only scholar who has done such similar research is C. W. E. Bigsby, who has an elaborate observation in the last chapter entitled "Redefining the center: politics, race, gender" in his *Modern American Drama, 1945-1990* (1992). Hence, this book intends to examine the unique version of the American dream in American ethnic drama. In addition to the primary focus on the relation between ethnicity and the American dream, the book will also employ four kinds of theorists' concepts to offer a new look at these plays. They are post-colonialist, post-structuralist, multiculturalist, and post-Marxist. The one universal characteristic shared by these four different theorists is their deep concern with the victimized (ethnic) group. First of all, post-colonial theorists Frantz Fanon in his *Black Skin, White Masks* and Edward Said in his *Orientalism* and *Culture and Imperialism* help analyze how whites' hegemony shapes the ethnic other and how the marginalized internalize the distorted image of themselves. Secondly, the notion of counter strategy in post-structuralist Michel Foucault's *Language, Counter-Memory, Practice: Selected Essays and Interviews* (1977) may offer an insight into how the minority undertake resistance to rebuild themselves. Thirdly, both multiculturalism theorist Charles Taylor's "The Politics of Recognition" (1994) and Frankfurt theorist Jurgen Habermas's "Struggles for Recognition in the Democratic Constitutional State" (1994) bring forth mutual acceptance and respect as a solution to multicultural and ethnic issues. Lastly, post-Marxists Earnesto Laclau and Chantal Mouffe's concept of radical plural democracy proposed in *Hegemony and Socialist Strategy* (2001) and many other books serve to accentuate the importance of cooperation inside and between racial groups, which is also a shared feature of all these three plays. Owing to the common concern for the new prospect of these ethnic writers' vision, these theorists might very well offer new ways for the interpretation of the ethnic groups' social adaptation and their pursuit of the American dream.

IV. The Representatives of African American, Asian (Chinese) American, and Hispanic (Chicano) American Dramas

To illustrate the unique significance of the American dream for non-whites, I focus my discussion on dramas of three ethnic groups—African American, Asian American, and Hispanic American. I chose these three ethnic groups because of their visibility. According to the 2004 American census issued by the American Census Bureau in February 2007, the biggest minority group in America is Hispanic or Latino, with a population of 41,870,703 people (14.6% of the total US population). The second largest minority group is African American with 34,962,569 people (12.7% of the total US population). The third largest minority group is Asian American with 12,471,815 people (4.2% of the total US population).[2]

I will discuss African American drama (*The Piano Lesson*) first instead of the play written earliest (*The Chickencoop Chinaman*) among the three because I would like to begin with African American drama so as to explicate the indispensable way to the fulfillment of the American dream for non-whites—coalition. August Wilson's play is therefore singled out for illustration in Chapter Two. Many diverse peoples comprise Asian Americans, including eighteen defined groups. However, in Chapter Three I take Chinese American playwright Frank Chin as a representative playwright for Asian Americans because Chinese is the largest group (23%) among the eighteen defined groups of Asian Americans.[3] Among the various defined groups of Hispanic Americans—Mexican, Puerto Rican, Cuban, Dominica, and Central American, Mexicans, occupying 63% of the total of Hispanic Americans, are the largest sub-group. Hence, Mexican American playwright Louis Valdez's play is the focus of the discussion in Chapter Four.

The Piano Lesson, the fourth of August Wilson's cycle plays about the

---

[2] Other minority groups include American Indians with 2,357,544 people (0.8% of the total US population), Native Hawaiians with 397,030 people (0.001% of the total US population), and Jewish Americans. For more information, see http://factfinder.census.gov.

[3] Except for Chinese, the other 17 defined groups include Asian Indian, Bangladeshi, Cambodian, Filipino, Hmong, Indonesian, Japanese, Korean, Laotian, Malaysian, Pakistani, Sri Lankan, Taiwanese, Thai, Vietnamese, Other Asian, and Other Asian, not specified. See http://factfinder.census.gov.

African American experience in the twentieth century, depicts the physical journey of Boy Willie Charles from the South to Pittsburg, from wanting to sell the family piano to forsaking this plan, as well as the spiritual journey from ignoring his ethnic background to recognizing his true identity. Having worked for the white boss for years, Boy Willie cannot let a farm of his own slip through his fingers when he is offered a chance to buy it after the white owner Sutter dies. In addition to the money he has saved, he intends to sell the antique family piano, which is now kept by his sister in Pittsburg. Although he knows about the high price his father paid to claim the piano from their former white owner's house, and although he knows well that the piano encapsulates the Charles family's history of three generations in its artistic engraving, he seems to recognize only the economic value of this musical instrument in his desperate pursuit of the American dream. However, because Sutter's ghost also wants to claim ownership of the piano, Berniece's house is now greatly disturbed by the ghost's presence. Finally, after the fight between him and Sutter's ghost with the help of the Ghosts of the Yellow Dog, said to be the avenging spirits of the blacks in connection with the train invoked upon the call of Berniece's piano playing, Boy Willie finally understands the importance of the piano and foregoes the plan of selling it. At the end of the play, he returns to the South with a conviction of making money with his own hands but not selling his past. In Chapter Two, I interpret the lesson Willie and his sister learn and how blacks should achieve their American dream by rebuilding their dignity from their denigrated history.

Like Wilson's *The Piano Lesson*, Frank Chin's *The Chickencoop Chinaman* highlights a Chinese American Tam Lam's physical and mental journeys, from San Francisco to Pittsburgh, from rejecting his ethnic roots and his father to accepting his ethnic background, his father, and even himself. Shooting a documentary of his idol, the black lightweight boxing champion, Ovaltine Jack Dancer, Tam plans to share his vision of success and to leave a name for his children to remember him by. Unlike Boy Willie in pursuit of wealth, Tam is more concerned with his name and fame in his pursuit of the American dream. He first comes to his childhood friend Black Jap Kenji's place in order to get ready for their visit to Ovaltine's father Charlie Popcorn the next day. Kenji's friend, Lee, who is at the time staying with him as a guest, soon discovers that this witty, sharp, and aggressive Chinese American visitor has an inferiority complex; Tam feels ashamed of his ethnic identity. In fact, all these characters have some problem with their ethnic background; in addition to Tam's inferiority complex, Kenji pretends to be black, Lee attempts to pass as white, and even another visitor who appears later, Tom, also unwittingly suffers from such identity confusion. Tam, however, is extremely distressed when Charlie Popcorn tells him the truth that Ovaltine has also made up a story to cast himself in hero's armor. Charlie Popcorn also sees through Tam's split personality problem and teaches him to see his father straight, whom Tam has despised but Charlie Popcorn has revered clearly. This disillusionment finally forces Tam to take himself as who he genuinely is. Finally, the defeat is replaced by a new hope when Tam in the kitchen is reminded of his grandfather, grandmother, and numerous Chinese railroad workers, embodied by the train "the Iron Moonhunter." Like the Ghosts of the Yellow Dog in Wilson's *The Piano Lesson* which used to run in the South and which had thus borne witness to African subjugation, the Iron Moonhunter also invokes a past when Chinese Americans were sweating for the making of America. In Chapter Three, I analyze how Tam, through the reconfirmation of the blacks and recognition of old Chinese railroad workers' contributions, rebuilds himself under the shadow of his father's (ancestors') subjugated past. Frank Chin finds a way for Tam to rehabilitate his disillusioned ambition, and this recognition is precisely how Chinese Americans should realize their American dream.

Luis Valdez's *Zoot Suit* is based on two real historical incidents, the Los Angeles Sleepy Lagoon Murder case of 1942 and the related Zoot Suit Riots of 1943. The play is a combination of *actos* (or "protest skits"), *mitos* ("myth"), and *corridor* ("ballad"), in which a group of *pachucos* (Mexican American gang members), led by Henry Reyna, are charged and sentenced with the murder of another Mexican American. "Distinguished" by their slicked-down hair and suits with long, exaggerated coattails, these young Mexican Americans are treated brutally by (white) LA police, cheaply exploited by the (white) media, and unjustly judged by the (white) judge and the jury on the grounds that Chicanos are subhuman. However, thanks to the assistance and encouragement of their white lawyer and community activists, Henry and his twenty-one men win the appeal and are released. By means of this docudrama, Luis Valdez presents the ugly past when the nation turned its xenophobic persecution toward the Chicanos during WWII. At the end of the play Valdez makes Henry mature after struggling between his desire to assimilate versus maintaining a Chicano subjectivity. After his blunt clash with white power, the Chicano hero forsakes his zoot suit, achieves self-control, and becomes proud of his Chicano family and heritage. This first Chicano play to hit Broadway, in fact, garners the merit of paying homage to Chicano cultural heritage and its *pachuco* myth. Hence, in Chapter Four I analyze the traumatic past of Mexican Americans, the internalized inferiority complex, and the new ethnic identity proposed in the play, which is a key to the fulfillment of their American dream.

Numerous books and journal articles have been devoted to *The Piano Lesson*, *The Chickencoop Chinaman*, and *Zoot Suit*, but few have placed these three together to explore how these characters of a similar immigrant setting rebuild their own subjectivity while searching for their American dream. None has pointed out the significance of solidarity and coalition inside and outside their ethnic groups. August Wilson, Frank Chin, and Luis Valdez did not have their lives converge in any matrix of time and space. Nevertheless, simultaneously they all bring forth an ethnic pride for their ethnic and white viewers. Wilson presents the black slave history myth, Chin uses the Chinese railroad workers' myth, and Valdez creates the defiant *pachuco* myth. Instead of feeling ashamed of their once-denigrated traumatic past, these ethnic playwrights want their fellow people to find strength and take pride in their ethnicity. In spite of entirely different ethnic backgrounds, the three share the same passionate concern over their own people's adaptation to the hegemonic white culture and society. What they present in their plays is discrimination from whites, the ethnic minority's internalization of self-loathing, the ignorance of their true worth, and an anxiety-over-assimilation complex. However, they offer the healing of the traumatic past, the understanding of their dignity, and a plea for recognition. They also advocate a new cross-ethnic frontline for the minority groups to gather together and magnify their power for success. The wish to bring back self-recognition and self-respect, and the request to have one's due respect, and to be free and equal to whites in America is the American dream shared by all the ethnic people of the modern diaspora in America.

Chapter Two

The American Dream for African America

in August Wilson's *The Piano Lesson*

I. Introduction

Among major American ethnic groups, African Americans are probably one of the two most afflicted minority groups in America.[4] According to scholars, from the seventeenth century in Africa, native Africans were captured by slave catchers, and they were chained together and marched long distances, often hundreds of miles, to the European forts near the coast and then they were forced onto ships headed for America (Banks 199). Because of the brutal treatment and inhuman conditions on board, "Some historians estimate that one out of every eight captives died in the middle passage and never reached the Americas" (Banks 200). Once they were in America, blacks encountered even harsher treatments, sold to be slaves toiling all their lives, their children forever slaves. "By the end of the seventeenth century, slavery existed in fact as well as in law in Colonial America" (Banks 200). Despite the fact that their legal status as slaves was abolished after the Emancipation Proclamation in 1863, blacks did not enjoy freedom and equality. As James A. Banks states, "American slavery was a unique

---

[4] The other major ethnic group is Native Americans, or American Indians. All the minority groups have suffered great pains adapting themselves to the new country; however, in my opinion, Native Americans (Native Hawaiians too) and African Americans have been through more miseries than other groups who have come to America willingly. Native Americans have been deprived of their land, life style, and culture. Many American Indians were extinguished through genocide. African Americans, as mentioned earlier, were forced to come. Many perished before their ships made it to America.

institution in human history that was designed to dehumanize Blacks and to convince them that they were inferior and deserved the treatment they received" (200). As a consequence, even after the Emancipation, this detrimental and demeaning ideology about blacks remained virulent and blacks were still exploited and discriminated against. Such racial inequality was not redressed until the Civil Rights Movement, or the Black Power Movement, in the 1960s.

Louis Althusser poignantly states that Repressive State Apparatuses are state sanctioned agents that regulate and discipline us "by violence" (145); however, Ideological State Apparatuses are more vehement tools in confining us because they condition our ideas and mindsets predominantly "by ideology" and secondarily "by repression" (145). Accordingly, because of attenuated, concealed, and symbolic functioning (145), ISAs can be thus more damaging to our views on people and life. As mentioned before, whites' subjugation of blacks continued after the Emancipation because it could "enable Whites to make maximum profits from Black labor and to reinforce ideals of supremacy" (Banks 201); whites not only exploited blacks but also justified their act of instilling into them the demeaning theory of black inferiority. This distortion has unfairly done a great damage to blacks in physical and spiritual aspects. Many black intellectuals feel it urgent and necessary to write their own history and rebuild their own image in their works. One can find such common concern in the legacy of African American drama in the works of Langston Hughes, Lorraine Hansberry,[5] Amiri Baraka, Alice Childress, and August Wilson.

---

[5] In many ways, Lorraine Hansberry (1930-1965) bears some resemblance to August Wilson. Her play, *A Raisin in the Sun* (1959), the first play by a black woman to be produced in Broadway, also discusses the American dream of African American. It is also a play about one black family's awakening consciousness "as they come to realize the effects on their own sensibilities and identities of internalizing the values of their society" (Bigsby, *Critical Introduction* 381-82).

Among these playwrights, August Wilson (1945-2005) certainly is the most prominent one because of his continuous dedication and contribution, his militant publicity, and his outstanding accomplishment.[6] He has also been acknowledged as one of the great dramatists in twentieth-century America. Many scholars have paid attention to Wilson's family background and his self-taught high school life.[7] Although he was born to a white German father and African American mother, Wilson had a strong identification with his mother's ethnic background, and he continued throughout his life championing blacks' rights and advancement.

Acclaimed as "America's Shakespeare" (*Oregon* 51), or the Bard, by theatrical professionals, Wilson has garnered countless praise for his project to write the decalogy that would chronicle the twentieth-century African-American experience.[8] Nevertheless, he rarely portrays controversial political events directly in his plays, believing that depicting ordinary blacks' daily life more relevant. At an interview with C. W. E. Bigsby, Wilson explains, "the plays... deal with those people who were continuing to live their lives. I wasn't interested what you could get from the history books" (Bigsby, *Modern* 287). In spite of his said

---

[6] Wilson is definitely the most significant African American dramatist. He has aroused great attention because of a ground-breaking record in the history of African American drama; that is, in 1988, he had two plays running simultaneously on Broadway—*Fences* (first performed in 1985) and *Joe Turner's Come and Gone* (1986). To be able to have prominent performances in white dominated Broadway marks a new history for the presence and eminence of African American culture.

[7] Wilson dropped out of high school at age fifteen after refusing to defend himself against false charges of plagiarism on a history paper. For further information about the life of August Wilson, see "August Wilson" in *Dictionary of Literary Biography*, or "August Wilson" in *Contemporary Author Online*, http://galenet.galegroup.com.

[8] For each decade of the twentieth century, Wilson writes a play. The ten plays are set in different decades: *Gem of the Ocean* (2004) set in 1904, *Joe Turner's Come and Gone* (1988) 1911, *Ma Rainey's Black Bottom* (1984) 1921, *The Piano Lesson* (1990) 1936, *Seven Guitars* (1996) 1949, *The Fences* (1987) 1957, *Two Trains Running* (1992) 1969, *Jitney* (1982) 1977, *King Hedley II* (2001) 1985, and *Radio Golf* (2005) 1997. For further information about Wilson's "haphazard" project, please see Philip D. Beidler's "King August: August Wilson in His Time," pp. 580-81.

belief, his plays are indicative of the positive impact of the Civil Rights Movement because embodied in his plays is a strong sense of pride in being black, which is the most crucial issue in resisting white racist distortion. Although Wilson endeavors to convey his views on African American aspiration in all the ten plays, *The Piano Lesson*, premiered in 1987, published in 1990, and the fifth of his ten-play decalogy, appears to carry a strong message to African Americans as is suggested from the title itself. It has also won the Drama Desk Outstanding New Play Award, the New York Drama Critics Circle Best Play Award, a Tony Award Nomination for Best Play, the American Theatre Critics Outstanding Play Award, and the Pulitzer Prize for drama.

Set in 1936 during the Depression, *The Piano Lesson* describes the journey of Boy Willie from the South to Pittsburg and his confrontation with his sister Berniece about selling their family piano to pursue his American dream. Boy Willie wishes to set up his own farm just like his former white plantation owner Sutter. The capital he relies on is the antique family piano passed down from his father at the expense of his life, now kept by his sister Berniece in Pittsburg. Regarded as the heirloom and history of their family's (African) past, the piano means more than its antique value, since it is carved with the stories about the life of Boy Willie's ancestors as slaves. After the battle of life and death with the Ghosts of the Yellow Dog against their white master bound in the piano, Boy Willie finally realizes the worth of his own afflicted past and learns to stand on his feet to raise money on his own to buy his farm. If he wants to own a farm, he has to first have a clear vision of what his American dream exactly entails. Wilson in this play does not discourage blacks from embracing their economic success; nevertheless, he warns them about being deluded by a kind of dream celebrated by whites but actually inappropriate for blacks at this stage.

II. The Misconceived Version of Whites' Material Dream

When the play begins, all the characters in *The Piano Lesson* have some awareness of the American dream they are seeking, but their dreams are all the misconceived version modeled after white's material dream. Major characters like Boy Willie and Berniece and minor characters like Avery, Lymon, Doaker and Wining Boy, are greatly influenced by whites' dream, which illustrates their unwitting assimilation. Lost in the material world, they place more emphasis on economic success than on spiritual needs.

A. Major Characters' Dreams

Boy Willie, a man working for white landowners most of his life, aspires to become a landowner, to be the master of his own farm. His aspiration is a good dream but at this stage he sees the material worth of everything, including his dream. The most expedient way to realize his dream is mainly by selling his family piano, i.e. selling out his ancestors' suffering past and ethnic pride. To fully grasp the spiritual value of his dream and to use a dignified way to make the dream come true is a lesson he needs to learn.

According to the stage direction, Boy Willie "is brash and impulsive, talkative and somewhat crude in speech and manner."[9] As suggested by his name, he is still boyish or idealistic in his concept of the American dream and in his understanding of how to realize his dream. At the beginning of the play, he straightforwardly announces his dream and his plan to carry it out to his uncle Doaker: "Sutter's brother selling the land. He say he gonna sell it to me. That's why I come up here" (9). Boy Willie has a simple dream—to buy the land he and his ancestors used to work on, and he has all the determination to pursue his

---

[9] *The Piano Lesson*, (New York: Plume, 1990), pp. 1-2. All subsequent references to this play will be noted parenthetically in the text.

dream. Among all the characters in the play, Boy Willie is the only one full of vitality, determination and action. He is also the only man who clearly knows what he wants to do. When he has a chance to realize his dream, he seizes it right away. He has three weeks to collect the money ($1500 to $2000). He also has a perfect plan to get his money: "I got one part of it. Sell them watermelons and get me another part. Get Berniece to sell that piano and I'll have the third part" (9). He has been working hard to save some money and is also quick in finding other capital, shipping watermelons to Pittsburg for sale and selling the family piano. Unlike the rest of the characters, he will not stay in the North, and he is going back to the South to work. He says, "I ain't scared of work. I'm going back and farm every acre" (17).[10] But he's now still unaware of how untried his American dream is and how he should better acquire his capital.

At this stage, Boy Willie, though endeavoring to improve his social life and status, still does not know how to connect his material dream with his ancestors' past. He may have a very correct and admirable idea of his or blacks' position and rights in this world, which will be further discussed in the following part, but his persistence to seek the material dream is so strong that he is blinded by the alluring material glamour of the dream and is willing to sacrifice his cultural heritage and dignity. When others are ruminating on the doleful past of the piano, he tells them that land is more useful than the piano:

> If my daddy had seen where he could have traded that piano in for some land of his own, it wouldn't be sitting up here now. He spent his whole life farming on somebody else's land. I ain't gonna do that.

---

[10] August Wilson in fact proposes that blacks stay in the South to engage in what they and their ancestors have known for hundreds of years—farming (Bissiri 4; Rothstein 2). Even if they remain in the North, Wilson maintains, they are "tied to the South" (Harris 370) and should still connect themselves to the South, and they should not forget about their agrarian life in the South (Plum 563).

See, he couldn't do no better. When he come along he ain't had nothing he could building on. His daddy ain't had nothing to give him. The only thing my daddy had to give me was that piano. And he died over giving me that. I ain't gonna let it sit up there and rot without trying to do something with it. If Berniece can't see that, then I'm gonna go ahead and sell my half. (46)

Boy Willie believes blacks toil their whole life only for the sake of the material provisions of life. He sees nothing but the exchange value of the land and the piano. He does not think highly of his father's sacrifice in securing the piano or the symbolic value of the piano; instead, he tends to be practical about the value of the piano. Hence, he would rather sell the piano, erasing the historical and ethnic significance of the piano. This warped vision about the piano and the past reveals the strong influence of the material American dream.

Whereas Boy Willie wishes to be a landowner, Berniece annihilates her subjectivity, projects her dream onto her daughter Maretha, and wishes her to be a minority model. After her husband Crawley has been shot by the white sheriff, Berniece moves to the North in the hope of staying away from the South, which is to her a place filled with endless killing and sorrow. In Pittsburg, she chooses to be evasive and submits herself completely to white domination by burying herself in a mourning mood and passivity. As a habitual and involuntary surrender to the blacks' doleful past, Berniece refuses to accept Avery's proposal, or rather, to change her life pattern.[11] Avery then questions her with this willful self-sacrifice by saying, "How long you gonna carry Crawley with you, Berniece? It's been over three years. At some point you got to let go and go on. Life's got all kinds of twists and turns" (66). Berniece's refusal to move on with life parallels blacks'

---

[11] The playwright seems to suggest that Berniece has indulged in such evasive self-pity by this excessive mourning because the stage direction for her first appearance instructs, "She is still in mourning for her husband after three years" (3). Indeed, she hardly considers the possibility of a second marriage.

passivity. As Harry J. Elam Jr. aptly points out, "Wilson depicts Berniece's commemoration of and mourning for Crawley as retarding agents restricting her progress in the present" ("Dialectics" 367). She in this sense buries herself in the white dominant northern city, erasing her subjectivity.

The same evasive mindset makes her alienated from playing the family piano. As Doaker says, "I ain't never know her to touch [the piano] since Mama Ola died. That's over seven years now" (10). She herself tells Avery, "I don't play that piano cause I don't want to wake the spirits" (70). Although she remains passive and aloof from the world, Berniece wishes her daughter to have a better life in this world. In other words, she projects her dream onto Maretha, a dream imbued with her assimilation ideology. As Doaker explains Berniece's plan to Boy Willie, Berniece "got Maretha playing on it though. Say Maretha can go on and do everything she can't do ... She wants Maretha to grow up and be a schoolteacher. Say she good enough she can teach on the piano" (10).

Berniece intentionally runs away from her family's past because she only sees the destructive part of it. She also deliberately keeps the past from Maretha: "[Maretha] don't know nothing about it. Let her go on and be a schoolteacher or something. She don't have to carry all of that with her. She got a chance I didn't have. I ain't gonna burden her with that piano" (70). Berniece simply wants Maretha to have nothing to do with her black ancestors and to forget her cultural roots. This indicates Berniece detests her ethnic roots and wishes to be like whites. Such self-hate is what Franz Fanon in his *Black Skin, White Masks* has effectively pointed out. In the chapter of "The Fact of Blackness" Fanon analyzes how blacks are locked in their "crushing objecthood" (109) and how they have to spend their life crawling, "being dissected under white eyes, the only real eyes" (116). "Shame and self-contempt" for themselves overwhelm blacks (Fanon 116).

Therefore, Berniece tells her daughter to hide her color when she is out (26) and she makes an effort to iron her daughter's curly hair into straight hair (89-90). This act to erase one of her (daughter's) black features is exactly how Fanon describes the mentality of the self-loathing Antilles—"Look, I will accept the lot, as long as no one notices me" (116). Berniece's behavior shows the deep impact of racist assimilation. "Because the cultural experiences of marginalized groups like African Americans have been interpreted by historians according to the values and ideals of a white male culture" (Plum 561), Berniece is accustomed to identifying with whites' ideology and looking down upon blacks' culture and history. Fanon in the chapter of "The Negro and Psychopathology" also explains how pervasive such inculcation is at school (147) and how powerful such collective unconsciousness is everywhere (188). Hence, it is only natural for Berniece to conceive that kind of white dream and to project it onto Maretha.

Neither Boy Willie nor Berniece has a viable vision of the American dream yet at this stage. Boy Willie internalizes the American capitalist dream and would like to realize his dream in exchange for his family piano and his ancestors' history of blood and tears. Berniece internalizes the white lens to view herself and her people and would like to project her dream onto her daughter making her a submissive black piano school teacher content about "staying low at the bottom of society" (94), ashamed of her skin color and oblivious to her ancestors' past.

B. Other Minor Characters' Dreams

Though not as important as the sister and the brother, the minor characters in *The Piano Lesson* also play a crucial part to illustrate Wilson's manifestation of the American dream of African Americans. Like Boy Willie and Berniece, the minor characters—Wining Boy, Lymon, Doaker, and Avery have their dreams greatly impacted by their white counterparts; they either look up to the capitalist dream or choose to embrace their assigned, subjugated lot.

Among the minor characters, Wining Boy and Lymon pursue a life of affluence in big cities, which is a capitalist dream more like Boy Willie's. Wining Boy, gifted in music, makes money by playing the piano; however, no matter how much he earns, he squanders it on gambling. Young and preoccupied with finding a mate, Lymon focuses on making quick money and spends it on getting a woman for him. As a critic notices, these two, who actually could be father and son, are more trapped by materialist temptations.[12]

While Wining Boy and Lymon are assimilated into whites' capitalist values, Doaker and Avery represent two other kinds of blacks deeply influenced by the dominant white discourse in their vision of the dream. Confronted with the debate between Boy Willie and Berniece over the piano, Doaker only stays away from it, refusing to have any say about it. "Ain't nobody said nothing about who's right and who's wrong" (46), defends Doaker. As Berniece tells Avery, "Doaker don't want no part of that piano. He ain't never wanted no part of it" (69). His philosophy of life is to remain passive and invisible, more like Berniece's escapism. When Boy Willie questions why he or Berniece has not told Maretha about the piano's story, Doaker replies, "I don't get in the way of Berniece's raising her" (22). When Boy Willie retorts against Berniece's theory of blacks living at the bottom of society, Doaker comments, "I'm just living the best way I know how. I ain't thinking about no top or no bottom" (93). When he sees Sutter's ghost in the house, he makes no noise about it and lives with it. Doaker's determination to mess with nothing attests to a very salient mindset of many

---

[12] Susan C. W. Abbotson derives from Wining Boy's recounting of Lymon's parents' affair that Wining Boy may very likely be Lymon's real father (87). The fact that Lymon buys the suit and shoes from Wining Boy and later dresses himself up in Wining Boy's outfit also strongly suggests a close resemblance, or tie, between these two men (Abbotson 87).

African Americans—passivity.

Avery is the most obvious example of assimilation. Beneath his dream to have a church of his own lies a black man who has been completely converted, physically and spiritually. After moving north into the big city, Avery has been working at a skyscraper running an elevator. He expresses his satisfaction with his job because it "got a pension and everything;" then he adds a further illustration, "They even give you a turkey on Thanksgiving" (23). Meanwhile, he was inspired in a dream and is now trying to get a loan to start his own church. Boy Willie detects some slave mentality in Avery's words when he tells about his determination to work his way up, not to be simply silenced at the bottom. He criticizes Avery's complacency: "Avery think cause the white man give him a turkey for Thanksgiving that makes him better than everybody else. That's gonna raise him out of the bottom of life. I don't need nobody to give me a turkey. I can get my own turkey" (93). As a contrast to Boy Willie's aspiration to define himself and to be on his own feet, Avery obviously appears to be too complacent leading a life whites assigned him to have. As in the case of Berniece, Avery is presented as a docile body and subject in a world dominated by whites' ISAs and RSAs.

Avery's dream to have a church of his own also reveals the playwright's distrust with Christianity, a religion set up by whites inculcating the black to be meek and humble even in their affliction. As Sandra Shannon contends, Christianity in Wilson's plays is often under interrogation because the ideology like the one in the Book of Job has been appropriated to teach blacks what "humility" is and to be subjugated without rebellion ("Good" 128).[13] Firstly, the

---

[13] Like many other African Americans who noted "that their white oppressors often quoted the scriptures to them to justify so-called 'ordained' subjugation," Wilson also maintains that "God does not hear the prayers of blacks" (Shannon, "Good" 127).

other black characters in the play seem to doubt Avery's motivation to serve God because they all deem the reverend's job an easy one as Lymon comments, "Avery say he gonna be a preacher so he don't have to work" (23). They have reasonable doubt because back home in the South "plain old" Avery never aspired to be a reverend. As Shannon has pointed out, they consider that "Avery is a shyster" and they don't believe he was "called" to the ministry, "choosing instead to believe that, like them, Avery has found a lucrative scheme to support himself" ("Good" 141).[14] Secondly, in his dream Avery was called by God and told to be shepherd for God's flock, and this is why Avery will name his church "The Good Shepherd Church of God in Christ." It is true that the Bible has the shepherd and the sheep as a metaphor for God or the church and the people. However, humility and subservience have also at the same time been used by the people at the top of society for those at the bottom of society. Hence, Avery's dream to start his own church to look after black souls is a not only a replica of whites' religion, but it is also an institution to inculcate whites' idea that blacks should be content with their life at the bottom. Not yet challenged by the big test, Avery as well as other minor characters all have misguided dreams.

III. The American Dream to Be Fulfilled by African Americans

When studying the American dream which motivated the Black Migration from 1915 to 1919, Cernkovich et al. discover that African Americans maintain a stronger commitment to the American dream than do Whites (Cernkovich et

---

[14] In the play Avery's pious vision and mission is marred by a story told by Wining Boy, in which a guy in Spear claimed to be Jesus Christ and attracted a huge crowd for his enactment of Jesus' life. When people gathered to see the part of crucifixion, he stopped everything and told people to go home and go to his church on Easter Sunday to celebrate his resurrection. Wining Boy thus comments, "I don't know who's the worse fool. Him or them" (30). This story indirectly satirizes people like Avery who think themselves justified to lead the people as a Christian (church) leader.

al.131). When a group of people is denied full access to the American dream, their attitude towards subscribing to the goals of economic and material success will not be as important as the goals of tolerance and respect. In other words, there are some elements that these ethnic groups look forward to more desperately. August Wilson in *The Piano Lesson* shows his audiences that the most pertinent and urgent concept when African Americans would like to realize their dream is to face their past, to be proud of their ancestors' suffering past, and to make efforts to win recognition and respect. Unfortunately, most African Americans have been acculturated and they look at their ancestors' past from a white perspective. It is this wrong attitude the playwright would like to redress in the cause of blacks realizing their American dream.

A. The Wrong Attitude towards the Past

The blatant message in the play, conveyed through the cheerful young man Boy Willie, is for blacks not to be ashamed of their past, but to embrace their past. As many critics argue,[15] the piano symbolizes the past, or the legacy. Berniece's attitude to turn away from the piano, not to touch it and not to tell its story, parallels most African Americans' attitude towards their ancestors' past, a past too humiliating and too miserable for them to look upon.

To Berniece, the piano is an embodiment of the family's sad history and she cannot make out why a piece of wood would cost many men's lives, which in turn afflict their women's lives. She draws the men's attention to its ominous significance:

> Look at this piano. Look at it. Mama Ola polished this piano with her tears for seventeen years. For seventeen years she rubbed on it till her hands bled. Then she rubbed the blood in […] you ain't never

---

[15] See Abbotson 83-84, 98; Boan 3; De Vries 25; Bissiri 29; Elam, "Dialectics" 374.

> stopped to look at what this foolishness cost your mama. Seventeen years' worth of cold nights and an empty bed. For what? For a piece of wood? To get even with somebody? I look at you and you'll all the same. You, Papa Boy Charles, Wining Boy, Doaker, Crawley … you're all alike. All this thieving and killing and killing and thieving and killing […] It don't never stop. (52)

With her mother's and her own miserable lives scarred in her mind, Berniece treats the piano as a piece of wood whose value is for men to exert their masculinity and self-worth and whose lot always brings misfortunes to especially the female members of the family. It is simply a burden too heavy for her to bear; consequently, she respects the historical value of the piano but she will never touch that piano.

Berniece sees the soul in the piano but she cannot bring herself to face the piano. Unlike his sister who refuses to remember and recognize how those blacks have died over the piano, Boy Willie looks straight into the lives accorded to the piano and has no sentimental indulgence in it. However, his excessive rational attitude amounts so strongly to practical calculation that he can sacrifice the piano for the capital he needs in order to purchase Sutter's land. When the practical brother is determined to sell his share of the piano, the sentimental sister tells him, "Money can't buy what that piano cost. You can't sell your soul for money. It won't go with the buyer" (50). When she insists on leaving the piano sit in the house just for looks, Boy Willie explains his view:

> The only thing that makes that piano worth something is them carvings Papa Willie Boy put on there. That's what makes it worth something. […] Now, I'm going to build on what they left me. You can't do nothing with that piano sitting up here in the house. That's just like if I let them watermelons sit out there and rot. I'd be a fool. (51)

From the viewpoint of utilitarianism, he thinks Berniece's leaving the piano there without playing it or giving lessons on it is but a waste. He thinks it is wrong for Berniece to only see the "sentimental" value of the piano because without its productive use the piano will not yield any profits. To him, the piano equals the key to buying Sutter's land which will guarantee land, crop, cash, seed and maybe more. In other words, Boy Willie has commercialized the piano. Boy Willie has a more open and positive attitude towards the piano's gloomy past than Berniece. But when it comes to weighing between his capitalist dream and disposal of the piano, his openness and grand talk about celebrating the life-and-death acquisition of the piano are completely shattered and replaced by his material aspiration.

In his desperate and determined search for the capital, Boy Willie sees only the cash value of the piano and sacrifices his family legacy. In addition to this wrong attitude towards the piano and blacks' ethnic legacy, there is also another misrecognition by Boy Willie, which is lightly censured by the playwright; that is, Boy Willie intends to sell the piano to a white collector of blacks' musical handicrafts. According to Doaker, "Some white fellow was going around to all the colored people's houses looking to buy up musical instruments" (11). In fact, it looks like this white buyer, like old-time slave owners making profits through black slaves' labor, is also making money out of blacks' ingenuity. We cannot know whether blacks' ingenious artistic talent will be made renowned through the white broker's marketing strategy or not; however, a parallel between the white slave owner and the white collector hints at a new kind of exploitation of blacks by whites.[16] Thus, the playwright suggests Boy Willie not only has the wrong

---

[16] This kind of exploitation is well depicted in another play by Wilson—*Ma Rainey's Black Bottom*. In this play, the blues singer Ma Rainey and her band musicians make a lot of money for their white bosses but the good profits do not bring any improvement of the white oppressors' racism.

attitude towards blacks' past, but he might very likely cause their ancestors' affliction to be exploited again in his wrong vision of the American dream.

The other characters' attitude towards the piano either resembles Boy Willie's or remains passive. Avery also sees the commercial value of the piano. Indeed, it was Avery who first sent for the white collector for appraisal because he was hoping that Berniece would help him start his church by selling the piano. Both Boy Willie and Avery tend to be practical about the use of the piano but the difference between them is that while Avery has no emotional attachment to the piano, Boy Willie has his family's story engraved or carved on the piano. This connection makes Boy Willie's attitude towards the piano appear to be even more cold, rational, utilitarian, and nothing else. As to Doaker and Wining Boy's attitude, they seem to be so passive that they don't want to be involved with the piano affair.

When analyzing the characterization of Doaker and Wining Boy, Susan C. Abbotson thinks that they "provide contrasts which emphasize their nephew's vitality" (91). But she disagrees with Corlis Hayes (253-254) and Kim Pereira (*August Wilson* 96) who think Doaker as a man "at peace with himself." I agree with Abbotson because they confuse peace with passivity. Doaker and Wining Boy have less a say in the disposal of the piano because the legitimate owners of the piano are the brother and the sister. Nevertheless, they once participated in the "thieving" act to move the piano together with Boy Willie's father from Sutter's house to his own. Now they renounce their claim to the piano, maybe because they belong to the older generation. However, facing Sutter's appearance in his house, Doaker prefers to first keep quiet. Later, when he finds Sutter's ghost is caused by the piano, he would rather have no piano in his house. Though they can talk about their past, these people prefer to have nothing to do with the piano, or the past, if it brings "troubles" to them. It is this wrong attitude the playwright would like the audience to forsake. Being evasive, being utilitarian, or being passive is incorrect when dealing with their family's past, or blacks' legacy.

B. The Right Attitude

Berniece comments, "Boy Willie ain't nothing but a whole lot of mouth" (26); however, August Wilson conveys his idea about the correct attitude towards the piano, the family legacy, and the blacks' past through Boy Willie. This kind of mixing positive and negative aspects in one character is Wilson's consistent technique of characterization.[17] Therefore, in this play we see Boy Willie and Berniece make biased judgments but both of them also have their points in defending their view with respect to the piano. Apparently Boy Willie's more celebratory and militant attitude towards the piano offers a stronger illumination because it is a new and necessary one for blacks to embrace no matter what dreams they pursue.

Instead of realizing the material dream, African Americans should first realize their spiritual dream. They should understand that without seeing straight and clearly what their spiritual dream is, they can never fully attain the material dream. To have their spiritual dream fulfilled, they have to recognize their past. "Pivotal to the theme of reunion in Wilson's plays is the underlying premise to which he constantly returns that the solutions for the future lie in the past" (Pereira, "Introduction" 5). Susan Abbotson also believes, "The past provides a sense of connection, both temporally and personally. Also, it assists in

---

[17] In his plays, Wilson likes to make his protagonists flawed with some blind spots and his low-born characters distinguished by their accidental remarks of wisdom. For example, Troy Mason in *The Fences* is rebellious against white subjugation but is blind to his own extramarital affair and his son's self-realization through playing college football. Another character, Gabriel in *The Fences,* Toledo in *Ma Rainey's Black Bottom,* and Citizen Barlow in *Gem of the Ocean* are also good examples of such characterization. By mixing the two opposite natures together, Wilson makes his characters more human and closer to us.

self-definition and offers empowerment to those who freely embrace it" (83). African Americans need to confront themselves; they should no longer have a sense of inferiority when looking inward.

As Abbotson observes, "All must come to terms with the piano, which symbolizes their past, in a way that will allow them to progress to a brighter future" (84). This can be well illustrated by the lesson Boy Willie imparts to his sister. Boy Willie first advises Berniece not to be ashamed of their ethnicity, then tells her to celebrate it. Wilson illustrates this claim—feeling proud of African Americans' ethnic background—through the incidence of Berniece ironing Maretha's hair. When Maretha utters, "Owwwwww" to indicate hurt, Berniece, who is ironing and fixing Maretha's hair, answers, "Be still, Maretha. If you was a boy I wouldn't be going through this" (90). Boy Willie thinks Berniece wrong to say such a thing to Maretha because it will only make Maretha feel bad. Likewise, it is useless to think it a misfortune to be born black, and it is even worse if blacks simply accept whites' idea that they should reside at the bottom of society without doing anything.

Boy Willie's attitude towards their ethnic roots is to embrace them, not to be ashamed of them. Wilson himself asserts, "Without knowing your past, you don't know your present—and you certainly can't plot your future" (De Vries 25). Boy Willie criticizes Berniece's not telling Maretha about the piano, "Like that's something to be ashamed of. Like she supposed to go off and hide somewhere about that piano" (91). Boy Willie, on the contrary, advocates a welcoming approach. He asserts,

> You ought to mark down on the calendar the day that Papa Boy
> Charles brought that piano into the house. [...] and every year when
> it come up throw a party. Have a celebration. If you did that

[Maretha] wouldn't have no problem in life. She could walk around
here with her head held high. (91)

This is the attitude Berniece should have about the piano—to cherish it and to feel
proud of it. It is also the attitude Maretha and all other blacks should have about
their ancestors' past and their ethnicity.

Similarly, blacks should not feel ashamed of themselves. Boy Willie
condemns Berniece's shame and escapism because such thinking and behavior are
self-denigration and self-denial. Disagreeing with Berniece's way to educate
Maretha, he explains, "You got her going out here thinking she wrong in the
world. Like there ain't no part of it belong to her" (91). Wilson himself has also
pointed out that blacks would do themselves good and give the world a great
contribution if they look at their past without humiliation. "If black folks would
recognize themselves as Africans and not be afraid to respond to the world as
Africans, then they could make their contribution to the world as Africans" (qtd.
in Bigsby, *Modern* 293). Indeed, African Americans should not feel ashamed of
their past or their ethnic background.

When Michel Foucault dissects history, he never trusts the legitimacy and
continuity of history. He criticizes traditional history and brings forth the concept
of effective history. In "Nietzsche, Genealogy, History," he particularly questions
the unity and absoluteness of traditional history and instructs us to read against
the grain. Inspired by Nietzsche's criticism, Foucault proposes genealogy for
people to read and write/right history. He believes that a knowledge of traditional
history "easily disintegrates this unity [...] It easily seizes the slow elaboration of
instincts and those movements where, in turning upon themselves, they
relentlessly set about their self-destruction" (153). He argues, "'Effective' history
differs from traditional history in being without constants" (153) and teaches us to

read into the interstice of such traditional history. This is his counter-memory against mainstream history, or the grand narrative. Furthermore, he detects three uses that oppose and correspond to the three Platonic modalities of history: the parodic, the dissociative, and the sacrificial (160). "They imply a use of history that severs its connection to memory, its metaphysical and anthropological model, and constructs a counter-memory—a transformation of history into a totally different form of time" (160). This counter-memory is how the marginalized or oppressed people whose history was silenced or distorted should approach their past. When white oppressors write history and prescribe it for both whites and blacks, that history is not the correct or authentic version for blacks. Blacks should resort to a more constructive way to revisit their past.

Such a new way to read history and to write/right history is what August Wilson has engaged in for years. In an interview Wilson laments, "The fact of slavery is something that blacks do not teach their kids—they do not tell their kids that at one time we were slaves. That is the most crucial and central thing to our presence here in America. It's nothing to be ashamed of. Why is it, after spending hundreds of years in bondage, that blacks in America do not once a year get together and celebrate the Emancipation and remind ourselves of our history?" (Savran 295-96). Wilson endeavors to instruct African Americans to face their past in a way totally different from the way whites see them. Therefore, in his plays he faithfully and positively presents ordinary blacks' life. As one critic notices, Wilson's counter practice works "by documenting and celebrating black historical experience and by showing that embracing the African spiritual and cultural heritage can bring individual and collective healing for people" (Little par. 1). This is the counter-memory strategy Wilson employs when he writes his plays and he wishes to let his fellow people know they should discard the self-hate and feel proud of themselves. African Americans should feel proud because the prosperous country all the Americans have today owes a tremendous debt to blacks' hard work, and their (ancestors') toil and struggle are worthy of respect.

Wilson reiterates the importance for blacks to recognize their past and to embrace their ethnicity. Furthermore, he also teaches them to fight for what they deserve. They should not allow whites to write, claim, or own their past. In *The Piano Lesson*, the one to execute the counter-memory strategy for him is Boy Willie. Boy Willie is the one who has a clear vision of fighting for his due share on his own feet without surrendering to whites' subjugation or ideology. His central belief at the current stage is to buy Sutter's land. He asserts, "Hell, the land is there for everybody. All you got to do is figure out how to get you a piece. Ain't no mystery to life. You just got to go out and meet it square on" (92). He is not only quite correct in pointing out anyone can work hard to fulfill his American dream, but he is also equally correct to point out Berniece's problematic way of educating Maretha. "If you teach that girl that she living at the bottom of life, she's gonna grow up and hate you" (92). What Berniece is doing is internalizing what whites think they should be. She tells her brother, "You right at the bottom with the rest of us;" however, Boy Willie retorts, "If you believe that's where you at then you gonna act that way. If you act that way then that's where you gonna be. It's as simple as that. Ain't no mystery to life" (92). Boy Willie is poignant in criticizing most blacks' voluntary self-denial and submission to whites' domination.

He keeps emphasizing that there is no "mystery" about such mandated domination, so blacks should not give up upon their life and they should try their best to fight for their share. While Berniece keeps quiet about her life at the bottom, Boy Willie rebels against such an allocation. When "The world say it's better off without [him]," Boy Willie retorts,

> Hell, the world a better place cause of me. I don't see it like Berniece. I got a heart that beats here and it beats just as loud as the next fellow's. Don't care if he black or white. Sometime it beats louder. When it beats louder, then everybody can hear it. [...] Some people get scared to hear a nigger's heart beating. They think you ought to lay low with that heart. Make it beat quiet and go along with everything the way it is. But my mama ain't birthed me for nothing. So what I got to do? I got to mark my passing on the road. Just like you write on a tree, "Boy Willie was here." (94)

In this proclamation, Boy Willie shows his determination to realize himself and to get recognition. Instead of laying low with the heart beating noiselessly, blacks should make efforts to show they are worthy of recognition and respect. Boy Willie might sound like a braggadocio, but he definitely touches upon the quintessential key to success for African Americans; that is, not to be afraid of defeat or even death. He states, "a nigger that ain't afraid to die is the worse kind of nigger for the white man. He can't hold that power over you" (88). Boy Willie names this "the power of death." Critic Harry J. Elam Jr. has pointed out that this incredible power totally subverts the whites' traditional concept of master/slave dialectics ("Dialectics" 373-75). With this mindset to defy even death, blacks should be able to change their old fate. However, *The Piano Lesson* also has an important message: to actualize their American dream—to get what they deserve and to win over recognition, blacks should also fight together.

IV. The Solidarity

A new teaching in the play is that blacks should not only fight but they should also fight together. Few critics have noticed that in this play Wilson has also indicated this very important concept of solidarity for blacks to realize their spiritual dream. The only two critics are Susan C. Abbotson, who points out in her conclusion that the brother and the sister have to be united (100), and Mei-Ling Ching, who only mentions in passing about the joint effort of brother and sister to exorcize the past (71).[18] I think this message of solidarity for the oppressed is an invaluable notion from this sagacious playwright. In addition to recognizing their past and to fighting for their respect, African Americans should fight together.

The ending of *The Piano Lesson*—the fight between Boy Willie and Sutter's ghost—best exemplifies Wilson's concept of fighting together. After Sutter is dead, his ghost begins to haunt the Charles family in Pittsburg to "claim the piano." It is very difficult for audiences who are accustomed to western realistic aesthetics to accept the fight between Sutter's ghost and Boy Willie, and at the end of the play, the Ghosts of the Yellow Dog.[19] However, most academic critics regard such a supernatural device valid so that history and culture can be restored and connected (Little par. 34). Moreover, scholars who have done research on black history and literature have found that in black literature, "history often assumes a mythic quality in order to respond to questions of identity raised by a history largely told by and focusing on whites" (Campbell 155). Hence, it is natural to see that African American history in many literary works has to be structured as a continuing relationship between the living and the dead (M. Morales 106).

August Wilson calls the spectators' attention to the fact that this symbolic

---

[18] In addition to these two critics' comments on working together, Amadon Bissiri also emphasizes the importance of the chorus, which is not exactly the same as solidarity. He uses the example of an occasion when Boy Willie starts singing and Lymon, Wining Boy, and Doaker join in. "In this way—through music, oral culture—they live out their identity, tell of "who they are," and preserve their culture" (Bissiri 11).

[19] The most violent and repulsive reaction came from the famous Jewish theatre reviewer Robert Brustein, who denounced such a supernatural device and called it "unplayable," "forced," and "contrived" (30). The bitter and harsh criticism also ignited a tense confrontation between him and Wilson that lasted for years.

wrestling between black (Boy Willie) and white (Sutter's ghost) can only be resolved by the cooperation of the brother and the sister in evoking their ancestors' spirits. Obviously, Sutter's ghost is overwhelming so Avery's Christian exorcism fails, and even the young and self-confident Boy Willie fails to defeat Sutter's ghost single-handedly. The fight begins when the ghost of Sutter, upon Avery's Christian exorcism, makes his presence felt and menaces Boy Willie by choking him. As Boy Willie struggles, he frees himself, and then dashes up the stairs. The stage direction instructs, "There are loud sounds heard from upstairs as Boy Willie begins to wrestle with SUTTER'S GHOST. It is a life-and-death struggle fraught with perils and faultless terror" (106). It is at this moment Avery gives up his assistance as a Christian reverend because he sees Boy Willie defeated. "Avery is stunned into silence" and he tells Berniece, "I can't do it" (106). Avery is not the only one stunned; Doaker and Wining Boy stare at one another in stunned disbelief, too. Seeing her brother pick himself up and dash back upstairs, Berniece, all of a sudden, realizes what she must do. I think "the power of death" mentioned earlier by Boy Willie and concretely embodied here affects Berniece. Furthermore, she has an epiphany because the stage direction writes, "It is in this moment, from somewhere old, that Berniece realizes what she must do. She crosses to the piano. She begins to play" (106). The music she plays is a repetitive, simple, but powerful improvisation evoking their parents and grandparents' help. As Jonathan Little states, the blues song Berniece plays is "redemptive and empowering" (par. 32). The spirits carved into the piano are released and "The sound of a train approaching is heard. The noise upstairs subsides" (107). The Ghosts of the Yellow Dog finally overpower Sutter's ghost thanks to Berniece's timely enlightenment. With their past and ancestors evoked, Boy Willie and Berniece finally succeed. In other words, this victory also indicates that, without Berniece, Boy Willie might not be able to survive.

The brother and the sister both come to recognize the power of the piano, and most important of all, "the piano must remain as a living symbol of the family's painful, yet proud heritage" (Anderson par. 4). As Yvonne Shafer states, "in the final moments [Boy Willie] and Berniece achieve a closeness which seemed impossible early in the play and the mystical ending gives the audience a sense of elevation and hope" (276). Wilson clearly shows that, through the ending of this play, both Boy Willie and Berniece have to acknowledge their ancestors' past and legacy and they have to fight together. Susan C. Abbotson, the only critic who brings forth the importance of cooperation, states, "A lesson the piano teaches this family is that they must be united before they can turn their former bondage into a full sense of freedom. The piano leads Boy Willie and Berniece to team together against their real enemy, Sutter, rather than fight each other" (100).

In *Hegemony & Socialist Strategy: Towards a Radical Democratic Politics*, Ernesto Laclau and Chantal Mouffe propose a new strategy for all the oppressed—alliance. These post-Marxist scholars revolutionize not only the concept of the working class but also the methodology the working class should undertake. They expand the base of the working class in present day capitalist society and call attention to the heterogeneity and fluidity of the working class, which should include all the oppressed in "mélange" (38). Moreover, when discussing new socialist movements, Laclau and Mouffe very clearly point out no social movements are monads; "each movement cannot be indifferent to what takes place outside it" (141). Analyzing the new social movement, they observe that "the forms of this struggle undertaken by anti-racist movements will in part pass through the autonomization of certain activities and organizational forms, partly through a system of alliances with other forces, and partly through the construction of systems of equivalence among contents of the different movements" (141). In other words, one has to work with others so as to gain power in one's struggle for "the two great themes of the democratic imaginary—equality and liberty" (164). Although Laclau and Mouffe place their argument on the large scale blocs, their theory of solidarity can also be utilized in the cause of blacks' American dream. If individuals work hand in hand, they should not be afraid of being discriminated against. Wilson himself strongly supports the idea of working together. In his famous but controversial speech "The Ground on Which I Stand," he concludes with an appeal "to work together to create a common ground and to use the universal truth-telling power of the theater to improve all lives across the lines of culture and color" (Little par. 47). Although he does not particularly stress solidarity, one finds this common tendency not only in *The Piano Lesson* but also in many of his other works.[20]

V. Conclusion

The symbolic lesson in *The Piano Lesson* is that all blacks have to know the true value of their history and their cultural heritage and they must all work together to actualize their spiritual dream first. Critic Jay Plum maintains,

> Wilson's dramaturgy challenges the secondary position of African Americans within American history by contextualizing black experiences and, in turn, creating an opportunity for the black community to examine and define itself. Rather than writing history in the traditional sense, Wilson "rights" American history, altering our perception of reality to give status to what American history has denied the status of "real." (562)

African Americans shouldn't use white aesthetics to look at themselves. Hence,

---

[20] For example, in *Joe Turner's Come and Gone*, Loomis achieves psychic unification and communal empowerment with Bynum's help (Little par. 26). Likewise, Citizen Barlow in *Gem of the Ocean* also gets redeemed through the help of Aunt Aster and three other blacks.

Wilson's way is to present in his play a genuine rendition and interpretation of African Americans. At the same time, he successfully shows us that blacks can have their own history independent of whites' value judgment and distortion. This act and this play offer a counter strategy against dominant whites' hegemony over history and subjugation. The autonomous power from Wilson and the black characters in *The Piano Lesson* should also enlighten all other marginal groups to give a voice to themselves. This is why the critic would regard Wilson a master transcending "the categorizing of 'black' playwright to demonstrate that his stories, although consistently about black families and communities, speak to the entire U.S. culture" (qtd. in Shafter 277).

August Wilson has a vision: he wishes that blacks can see that their American dream can only be fulfilled through two praxes: one is to eradicate the distorted self-image imposed by whites, to rebuild themselves; the other is to do the regeneration/reconstruction job together. Highly inspired by the 1960s Black Power Movement (Ambush 581), Wilson has a strong conviction in blacks' power. Indeed, blacks are powerful people. But many blacks still do not recognize this point. Therefore, Wilson uses his drama to instruct them that blacks not only need to exorcize the white spell and rebuild their own self-value, they also need to work together. The famous historical event of 200,000 people participating in the March on Washington for Freedom and Jobs in 1960 and the success in boycotting racist buses across the States in 1960 precisely reaffirm the immensity of black power. With these events and many more in his mind, Wilson in *The Piano Lesson* imparts a critical message for blacks—to stand up to fight together, if blacks wish to realize their American dream.

Chapter Three
The American Dream for Chinese America in
Frank Chin's *The Chickencoop Chinaman*

I. Introduction

Different from African Americans whose ancestors were captured and shipped to become slaves, Asian Americans came to America of their own free will, seeking a chance to realize their own American dream. Although recent archeological finds have led to the speculation that the West Coast of America has been visited by Buddhist missionaries from China in the fifth century, and although direct evidence has proved that Chinese ship builders brought by the Spanish had visited Baja California as early as 1571 (Fong, "History" 13), most scholars still maintain that the immigration of Asians to the US has approximately 150 years of history (Chan 3; Min 7), or 200 years of history (Danico and Ng xiii). According to Pyong Gap Min, a large number of Chinese laborers moved to California from 1850 to 1882, and this is regarded as the first wave of Asian immigrants in the United States (7). Suchen Chan also asserts, "During the second half of the nineteenth century and the early decades of the twentieth, almost a million people from China, Japan, Korea, the Philippines and India emigrated to the United States and to Hawaii" (3). Chan in her book *Asian Americans: An Interpretive History* also lucidly points out the reasons for the influx of these groups of Asian immigrants. For example, "For Chinese, the first to arrive were pushed out by powerful forces at home as well as attracted by the discovery of gold in California, the Pacific Northwest, and British Columbia and by jobs that became available as the American West developed" (Chan 3).

However, their experiences in this country were far from allowing them to realize their dreams. As one scholar comments, "the United States is a nation that proclaims to welcome and assimilate all newcomers. But the history of immigration, naturalization, and equal treatment under the law for Asian Americans has been an extremely difficult one" (Fong, *Contemporary* 14). As aptly put by Ronald Takaki, Asians were "strangers from a different shore" (472). These strangers were "pushed" because "poverty hurt," but they were also "pulled" to "meet the labor needs of America's railroads, plantations, mines, farms, and factories" (Takaki 472). From the very start, or even before they came in numbers, they had been discriminated against by whites due to the whites' feelings of superiority. As Chan states, "like the indigenous populations of Hawaii, Alaska, and the continental United States pushed aside by Euro-Americans who desired their land, like Africans enslaved and condemned to hard labor in the New World, like Mexicans conquered and subjugated, Asians were deemed members of 'inferior races'" (45).

As mentioned in Chapter One, Chinese Americans are singled out among the Asian groups for the discussion of the American dream for Asian Americans in this book. Scholars have found that "the racially distinct Chinese were the primary scapegoats for the depressed economy in the 1870s, and mob violence erupted on several occasions through to the 1880s" (Fong, *Contemporary* 14).[21] Morrison G. Wong divides the history of Chinese American immigration into four phases from 1850 until now: Era of Antagonism (1850-1882), Era of Exclusion

---

[21] Fong in *The Contemporary Asian American Experience: Beyond the Model Minority* has a thorough account of the massacres of Chinese in 1871 and 1885. For more detail, see Chapter One, pp. 10-35, and especially "Anti-Asian Laws and Sentiment," pp. 14-16.

(1882-1943), Token Immigration (1943-1965) and Open Chinese Immigration (1965-present).[22] Except for the last phase, the names of the three eras all designate this history "characterized by episodes of prejudice and discrimination; of racism, xenophobia, and exclusion" (M. Wong 110). Scholars have recorded the dire history of these sojourners and immigrants' sweat, tears, blood, and death.[23] All in all, they came with the American dream at the inception; however, the American dream has later turned itself into an American nightmare. The nightmare has kept haunting their offspring because even if the inhumane laws have been abolished, the long lasting "chicken" image of Chinese American still has a strong grip on these people.[24]

Dawn fortunately came upon this dark history in the 1960s. Partly due to the prevalent anti-authority atmosphere, but principally due to the inspiring Black Power Movement, many marginalized groups or ethnic groups took actions to voice their discontent and to claim their history and rights. According to Mary Yu Danico and Franklin Ng, "Since the late 1960s, activists have tried to create an Asian American movement" (67). [25] These activists hoped to promote understanding of Asians in the United States and to empower their communities. They made efforts to destroy stereotypes and to replace them with authentic and positive images. Furthermore, that Chinese and other Asian groups have helped

---

[22] For further reference, see M. Wong's chapter "Chinese Americans" in *Asian Americans: Contemporary Trends and Issues*, pp. 111-116.

[23] Te-hsing Shan in his *Inscriptions and Representations* has a clear account of Chinese American history. See Chapter "I Was Ashamed to Be Curled up Like a Worm on Island," pp. 31-88. For more Chinese American history in English, see also Sucheng Chan's *Asian Americans: An Interpretive History* and *Entry Denied: Exclusion and the Chinese Community in America*, Stanford Lyman's *Chinese Americans*, and Mark and Chih's *A Place Called Chinese America*.

[24] For the reference to the discriminatory law, see also Shan, p. 47.

[25] For more information about this Asian American movement, see William Wei, *The Asian American Movement* and Steve Louie and Glenn Omatsu, eds., *Asian Americans: The Movement and the Moment*.

build America is also an undeniable fact. As Fong contends, "the Chinese were involved in many occupations that were crucial to the economic development and domestication of the western region of the United States" (*Asian American* 13). But this history of Chinese/Asian has long been neglected. Therefore, in the 1960s, Asian Americans began to claim their time not only in political action but also in the literary arena. It is in such a social-political content "of heightened awareness of ethnic identity and an increased sense of ethnic pride" (Chua 179) that Frank Chin began his dramatic career.

When Frank Chin's name is mentioned, many Chinese American scholars will soon remember his "unapologetically defiant voice" (Goshert 45) and the polemics he engaged in against popular Chinese American writers, Maxine Hong Kingston, Amy Tan, and David Henry Hwang.[26] In comparison with his opponents' oeuvres, Chin's writing is studied less and he is apparently neglected. As David Leiwei Li claims, this negligence is typified "by the institutional ignorance and the consequent under-read status of his works" ("Formation" 211). In fact, Chin does deserve more respect and study for three reasons. First, he has become one of the most diverse of all Asian American authors.[27] Second, he has spent his adult life reconfiguring the Chinese American male and rebuilding the Asian American man's self-esteem, which was distorted by white Americans and Western culture.[28] Third, his play *The Chickencoop Chinaman* was the first

---

[26] For the fight between the editors of *Aiiieeeee!: An Anthology of Chinese and Japanese Writers* (1974), and Maxine Hong Kingston, Amy Tan, and David Henry Huang, see King-Kok Cheung, "The Woman Warrior versus the Chinaman Pacific: Must a Chinese American Critic Choose between Feminism and Heroism?".

[27] Chin has published two novels, a volume of short stories and a collection of essays. He also co-edited two groundbreaking anthologies, *Aiiieeeee!: An Anthology of Asian-American Writers* and *The Big Aiiieeeee!: An Anthology of Chinese and American Writers*.

[28] It is admirable that Chin, a Chinese American, has worked persistently to redress the wrongs done to Japanese Americans and even Japanese Canadians during World War II. He has

Chinese American play produced off Broadway in New York in 1972.

Born in 1940, Frank Chin grew up in the San Francisco Bay Area and began his interest in writing in his college years in Berkeley and Santa Barbara.[29] Winning the 1971 East-West Players Playwriting Award, *The Chickencoop Chinaman* appeared Off Broadway at the American Place Theatre in 1972 and "established Chin's prominence in ethnic American literature" (Goshert 46). Although it is a play about the protagonist's journey to find his identity, Frank Chin in *The Chickencoop Chinaman* depicts the invisible but detrimental psychological state of Chinese Americans.

Meant to write against the grain, *The Chickencoop Chinaman* offended mainstream white play reviewers and received mixed reviews. As Keith Lawrence and John Dye comment, some reviewers of the play "tended to dismiss the play as a marginally interesting ethnic work that was ill formed and rhetorically unsound" (par. 11); meanwhile, others regarded it as a moving, funny, sarcastic, bitter play.[30] Later scholarly criticism is characterized by mixed but more objective estimation of the plays. Generally speaking, on the one hand, scholars like Elaine Kim and

---

recounted the tension between the official and unwritten histories of Japanese internment in his book, *Born in the USA: A Story of Japanese Americans, 1889-1946* (2000) (Maeda 1080). Chin organized the 1st Day of Remembrance to commemorate the incarceration of Japanese Americans during WWII (Shimakawa 61-62). Another incident that impressed me was his vehement verbal defense against the charge against Chinese man's passivity at a Conference called "Frank Chin and Asian Americans: Three Decades of the Artist: A One-Day Symposium Celebrating the Literature of Asian Americans" at Chinese Culture University in Taipei, 2005, which I also attended. During a discussion when Ms. Linda Arrigo made some remarks on the passivity of Chinese men, Frank Chin, who was 65 years old then and had experienced a stroke not long before, burst out with a fierce retort to defend against her stereotypical "white" observation.

[29] After studying for three years at the UC Berkeley, Chin participated in the Writer's Workshop at the University of Iowa from 1961 to 1963, and completed his degree at the UC Santa Barbara.

[30] For example, while white reviewer John Simon contemptuously entitled his review as "Hardly the Bother," another reviewer Michael Feingold admired the "good writing, well-caught characters, and sharply noted situations" (Lawrence and Dye par. 11). For more information about the play reviews, see Lawrence and Dye, "Frank Chin."

Michael Soo Hoo are perplexed by Chin's depiction of Asian American manhood; on the other hand, scholars like Sau-ling Wong and Patricia Chu see great value in Chin's condemning the negative white racist impact and Chin's success in mapping the Asian American male psyche.[31] Recent scholarly works such as David Leiwei Li's *Imaging the Nation: Asian American Literature and Cultural Consent* (1998) and Daniel Y. Kim's *Writing Manhood in Black and Yellow: Ralph Ellison, Frank Chin, and the Literary Politics of Identity* (2005) are more inclined to excavate the strengths of Chin's politics of Chinese American identity. In this chapter, I argue the ultimate message implied in this play is very crucial: self-recognition and self-respect, instead of self-loathing, escape, and substitution, are two keys for Chinese Americans to the fulfilling of the American dream.

II. The American Nightmare Manifested in *The Chickencoop Chinaman*

Chin in *The Chickencoop Chinaman* presents a Chinese American's pilgrimage to a black boxing champion's father. Behind his slick defense and tough appearance, the protagonist, Tam Lam, is vulnerable because he has internalized white racism. Tam and his childhood friend, BlackJap Kenji, have transferred their inferiority complex to worship Ovaltine Jack Dancer, a boxing champion, ever since they were boys. Tam not only has filmed the success of Ovaltine but also intends to include in the documentary the man behind the hero, Ovaltine's father, Charley Popcorn. However, instead of meeting a bigger-than-life father, Tam sees Charley, a porno movie house owner, and is told that he is not Ovaltine's father and the touching stories about the encouraging father and his tough training are all lies. Despite his dislike of Chinese, Charley tells him it is wrong to turn his back on his father and he even respects Tam's

---

[31] For detailed literature review on the play, see Lawrence and Dye, "Frank Chin," and Daniel Y. Kim, *Writing Manhood in Black and Yellow: Ralph Ellison, Frank Chin, and the Literary Politics of Identity*, pp. 163-65.

father more when he realizes who Tam's father is. At the end of the play, Tam learns to see himself without any illusion and to embrace himself, his forebears, and his ethnic background. Like a journey to self-understanding, Tam has to move from the two time spaces—the past of humiliation and self-loathing and the present of escape and substitution, before he can finally be on the right track to the fulfilling of his American dream.

A. The Past: Humiliation and Self-loath

Instead of the American dream, many ethnic writings call attention to the American nightmare (Hume 9). Similarly, *The Chickencoop Chinaman* does not seem to present any foreseeable American dream for the characters in the inception of the play. Instead, they encounter the American nightmare and it is derived from their humiliating past, which in this play is constituted by Tam's roots and his father. Tam is ashamed of his roots as a Chinaman, which is associated with culture: willowy, feminine, and "chicken." The play is replete with the allusions to the "chicken" or "hen" image of Chinese in America: notorious (7), submissive (13), nice and quiet (18), chicken (24), etc. [32] Chinamen have a sordid past (17) and their past is humiliating for manhood (26).

But all these images are distorted. In fact, what lies behind such malignant distortion of not only Chinese but also other Asians is a strong sense of the fear of the Orient and White supremacy; hence, scholars find that six images—the pollutant, the collie, the deviant, the yellow peril, the model minority, and the gook, portray the Oriental as an alien body and a threat to the American national family (Robert G. Lee 8). Chin himself and Jeffery Paul Chan particularly challenge such stigmatization to represent Chinese American men as "womanly,

---

[32] Frank Chin, *The Chickencoop Chinaman and The Year of Dragon* (Seattle and London: U of Washington P, 1981). All subsequent references are noted parenthetically in the text.

effeminate, devoid of all the traditionally masculine quality of originality, daring, physical courage, creativity" ("Racist Love" 68). Scholars have pointed out white ideology has this womanizing tendency to marginalize Chinese males to the effect that Chinese American men are deemed as castrated. King-Kok Cheung points out that whites simply construct Chinese American history in such a feminizing way that men suffer throughout their life ("Woman" 114). Therefore, to Chin and other coeditors of *Aiiieeeee!*, "emasculation" is "one of the most damaging stereotypes about Asian Americans" (Chin et al. xxx).

With this kind of distorted and negative ethnic image, Chinese Americans certainly have self-loathing. Neither can they identify with such ancestral images of humiliation. Many theorists, especially those working on Postcolonialism, like Franz Fanon, Edward Said, Homi Bhabha, and many others, all contend that white Euro-Americans tend to see their racial other in a denigrating lens, through which the ethnic groups negatively view themselves.[33] Non-whites in America and Britain, and the colonized in the colonial world suffer from both the institutionalized subjugation and internalized inferiority complex. In the context of Chinese American history, it is also easy to see how early Chinese laborers and settlers were ill treated, humiliated, and discriminated against in the strange and hostile land. Therefore, in addition to being ashamed of his ethnic history, Tam in the play is also ashamed of his father. Tam's father never appears in the play but from Tam's ambivalent perspective, his father is a "crazy isolated old" man (17). Because his father used to be a dishwasher, Tam never publicly acknowledges him as his father and he simply admits he has a "lousy father" (23). Although he has once protested that nobody respected his father like him (46), what Tam professes

---

[33] See for example Fanon's *Black Skin, White Masks*, p. 18, p. 210, Said's *Cultural and Imperialism*, Bhabha's *The Location of Culture*, Albert Memmi's *The Colonizer and the Colonized*, p. 105, David Lloyd's "Race under Representation," p. 70.

is altogether a stronger abomination than love or respect towards his father.

It is apparent to see that since the humiliation of and disgust toward his roots and father are so strong, Tam is ashamed of himself. Despite his outward aggressive, glib, and protective demeanor, he is quite weak in his mind. When provoked by Lee, BlackJap Kenji's visitor, a Chinese American passing for white, he shows his vulnerable part. Lee questions him, "Can't you fight? Why can't you get mad?" (25). Lee's confrontation illustrates why the passivity of Chinese Americans is taken to be their lack of masculinity. When in the surrealistic Limbo scene when Tam is unconscious due to physical breakdown and when he dreams of being on Popcorn's back recounting being abandoned by his wife on his birthday, he also cites his mother's words to comfort him: "My mother called and said she was proud I was taking it so well, and never asked if I was going to fight" (52). In brief, whites' racist ideology about emasculated Chinese Americans has a strong grip on Tam; he not only internalizes such a constructed negative self-image but also becomes paralyzed and emasculated under its charm.

In addition to Tam, almost all the other characters in this play suffer from this self-loathsome image. BlackJap Kenji has to erase his Japanese background by picking up an African American accent, lifestyle, and identity. Lee never tells people she has Chinese blood, continuously maintaining her white status while initiating relationships with men of different racial backgrounds. Tom thinks he has passed that stage of self-hatred because "We used to be kicked around, but that's history... Today we have good jobs, good pay, and we're lucky. Americans are proud to say we send more of our kids to college than any other race. We're accepted. We worked hard for it. I've made my peace" (59). He seems to be very complacent with his status of model minority. But somehow he still needs to marry a "white" woman (Lee) to feel secure. Furthermore, Tom's pride in his status as model minority is also highly susceptible to another form of self-loathing. In Daryl J. Maeda's view, Tom is an "assimilationist," whose model minority discourse as a palliative to racism is unambiguously rejected by Chin (1084). Ovaltine too needs to talk big and to fake a hero father to bolster his image. All these people have a lack in their identification. They fill up the lack with some strategic evasion, which only proves to be some disturbing nightmares to their life. Their nightmares are in this way inextricably connected to a humiliating past.

B. The Present: Escape and Substitution

The easiest way for these minorities to deal with their humiliating past is to forget it and to have a "better" substitution for an ignominious history. When Tam tells Lee about the adaptation of Chinese in America, Tam mentions once he asked an old man how stranded Chinese American men were, the man only told him it was no good for him to know such things, to let all that stuff die with the old (26). The old man tells Tam to forget it, "to get along with Americans." Very similar to African Americans' attempt to forget their past, as mentioned in the previous chapter, this old Chinese American, very possibly Tam's father, also chooses to forget the past. Like Berniece in *The Piano Lesson*, this old man only sees the shameful and doleful part of the past. Not only does the old man advise Tam to forget about the past, but Tam himself also wants his children to forget him. "I don't want'em to be anything like me, or know me, or remember me. This guy they're calling 'daddy'... I hear he's even a better writer than me" (27). Tam discredits himself and seems to feel "better" that his children now have a better "white" father. He intentionally buries the past of his ancestors, his father, and himself. In a sad self-derision, he says, "I've failed all the old men that ever trusted me. Sold 'em out, watched 'em die, lost their names..." (62). Tam tries to disclaim this line of Chinese American history. But in the deepest part of his heart, he knows oblivion does not help.

Forgetting the past is tantamount to one way of escapism, and replacing the shameful image with a virile projection is another way of escapism. However, while forcibly forgetting his Chinese past is ineffectual, faking a non-Chinese identity proves to be equally unsettling. Like BlackJap Kenji, Tam has picked up blacks' accent, partly because he went to school where assuming blacks' way of talking was a survival tactic, and partly because his idols are black (boxers). He could also take up different accents and styles of talking so deftly that he can easily fool a native black like Charley Popcorn on the phone or arouse boisterous laughter from people. He is obsessed with the power of words and is anxious about having no legitimate language of his own. Thus, he can take up any accent (Charley Popcorn takes him to be black) and can excel in any language (The Lone Ranger praises his well-spoken English).

No matter how he escapes from his contemptuous past and identity, Tam has to face the lack. Tam then fills up the lack by substituting other heroic figures so that he can have strong identities to look up to. The Lone Ranger, Ovaltine, and Charley Popcorn, though later prove to be disturbing and problematic, are the three heroes he embraces. Tam worships the Lone Ranger and thinks him a hero trotting alone in the West helping the poor. Ovaltine seems to embody Tam's American dream, a black ethnic single-handedly rising to the championship. He is not the macho type since he once won in the lightweight game, his stature not unlike the small-sized Chinese. Ovaltine's alleged father Charley Popcorn wears the heroic glamour because he is the one who "made" the hero. These three substitutions, however, will soon be shattered.

III. The Fulfilling of the American Dream Promised in *The Chickencoop Chinaman*

A. Recognition and Respect

Tam's aversion to his Chinese background makes him end up with nightmares; forgetting or evading is impossible and substituting is merely illusory. The Lone Ranger, Ovaltine, and Charley Popcorn all prove to be quite subjective projections. They are not true heroes for Tam to model because all of them not only have their problems but also deviate far from Tam's search for true identity and self-realization. Though like John Wayne the Cowboy in the West as representation of masculinity (Wang 38), the Lone Ranger is in fact a representation of the white racism, particularly mean in commanding Tam to preserve his "culture" (37). He even shoots Tam in his hand in Tam's dream, which can then be regarded as Tam's symbolic castration by whites. Ovaltine is a one-time champion, but he fakes his own past in order to be worshipped, ostensibly a concretization of his inferiority complex and lack of confidence. Charley Popcorn blatantly admits his dislike of Chinese, admits that he has no blood relationship with Ovaltine, and discloses no such heroic training fabricated by Ovaltine; namely, he is no hero maker. In a nutshell, no heroes are to be found, the substitutions are all defective, and some are even seriously flawed.

Act Two of the play serves as a journey of disillusionment, in which Tam confronts the validity of his hero substitutions and experiences his introspection. First, in his dream, he is disillusioned when he finds behind the mask of the Lone Ranger that it is racism that subjugates Chinese Americans. Then at Popcorn's porno house, his hope to pass on to people like him and his children an inspiring story of a self-made hero and the man behind the hero is crushed. Although the empowering substitutions are disempowered, Tam, among the debris of ruined hope, is forced to face his fake dreams, and particularly, to reevaluate his understanding of his father. In Limbo, he reminiscences and ruminates the most frustrating failure of his life—his divorce. He loses confidence in himself completely because this "marrying out" (marrying a white woman to prove to be whites' equal) to fill up his lack, fails. Moreover, like what Lee has pointed out, Tam did not do anything to win his ex-wife back because "[he] was taking it so well" (52). No wonder he laughs at himself to say all he can do is talk, not fight. "IT'S TALK. ALL TALK. NOTHING I CAN'T TALK.... BUCK BUCK BAGAW. BUCK BUCK BAGAW" (52). He knows he is an imprisoned hen, not even a rooster, which only crows but does not fight.

This recognition from disillusionment propels Tam to see for the first time why he used to escape from his roots, why he disowns his father, and why he feels ashamed of himself. But more importantly, he also learns from Charley Popcorn what others think about his father, a father so unlike his recognition in the past. Unlike critic Daniel Y. Kim who thinks Tam in his closing monologue at the end of the play "has begun to transform himself from the man he was at the beginning of the play" (196), I argue that Tam has begun to change himself when Charlie Popcorn discloses a story about Tam's father and reprimands him for his bad attitude towards his father. Charlie Popcorn knows Tam's father because his father used to go to watch Ovaltine train for fights. He says he could see the whole life of this "old Chinese gentleman" even though they couldn't really communicate. Once Charley Popcorn and Ovaltine wanted to let the old man in for free so Popcorn returned his dollar back to him. Popcorn recalls, "but he didn't understand, see. Me and Ovaltine didn't know that, and pointed in side, but he musta thought we were kicking him out. And he got this look on his face, he held up his dollar, and we shook our heads, telling him, you know, he was free. Then he said, I'll never forget it, 'Too moochie shi-yet.' And he walked away. I felt awful. I chased him down the street and held out my hand, and he gave me the dollar and I took him into the gym again. He had to pay. He would not be free" (44). Popcorn emphasizes, "But I liked to died, when he fierce, fierce! 'Too moochi shi-yet!' like that. Then I could see his whole life" (45). Popcorn does not go into detail to explain what life he speculates on, but we can guess that this Chinese gentleman not only had but also persisted in maintaining his principles. What is significant about the story of Tam's father is twofold. First, it is a story not narrated through the mouth of Tam's father, but a third-person unrelated to Tam's father, which validates its objective credibility. Second, through Charlie Popcorn's vivid narration, Tam's father is depicted in a positive and defiant perspective. This fierce little old Chinaman gave Popcorn an indelible impression. Tam then also understands why his father liked to be called "Chinatown Kid" because it was a nickname given by Charley Popcorn and Ovaltine. Tam remembers clearly his father "loved to be called that Chinatown Kid stuff too" (45). Now he knows this name is not pejorative but honorable. The once slighted name now connotes a rich significance to Tam.

A major reason that critics have regarded this play as a search for the ideal father (Chu 72; McDonld xiv) is also because this surrogate black father helps rebuild the image of the Chinaman father once rejected by Tam. This black mentor-father reassures Tam his father was a man of dignity and reminds him not to feel ashamed of his father. When Popcorn learns this old Chinese gentleman was Tam's father, Tam tries to evade the talk as usual by feigning that he was not his father, claiming, "He wasn't my father. He was... he was our dishwasher" (45). Popcorn immediately retorts, "What's wrong with dishwashers?" Popcorn soon perceives Tam's inferiority complex and his distorted recognition of his father. He impressively states, "No, this old Chinese gentleman wasn't scared. He had dignity" (46). While Tam gets oversensitive about Popcorn's comments, Popcorn poignantly emphasizes, "I don't think you should forget the old man." He confesses "colored people don't particularly favor Chinese" and with insistence on his honesty, he blatantly points out, "I think maybe I respected him more than you." The meaning of this remark dawns upon Tam. He is forced to answer the question of whether he respects his father or not. Although he defends himself saying, "No one respected him more than me" (46), he knows he is not certain about his self-defense.

In addition to Charlie Popcorn's enlightenment, another character's appearance also assists in Tam's bildungsroman and leads to his taking action. In the last scene Tom, a Chinese intellectual who comes to ask Lee to go back to live with him again, helps Tam re-assure his respect towards his father and himself. As suggested by the name, Tom is Tam's alter ego, though Tom himself has his own self-deception and blind faith. Thinking himself a Chinese who has passed the stage of self-loathing and who has been accepted by the white majority, Tom repeatedly accuses Tam "of being prejudiced against Chinese" (58; 59). Like Charley Popcorn pointing out his dislike of his father, Tom also charges Tam, "Now maybe you don't like being Chinese and you're trying to prove you're something else" (59). This reiteration of admonishment incenses and hurts Tam because Tam does have a strong inferiority complex. This is also why when he finds Tom's self deception of believing Lee to be white, Tam begins to lash out at Tom with his vehement and vicious verbal display, only to be checked by Kenji. All of a sudden, when challenged by his best friend, Tam confesses his tiredness of everything, particularly talking (62). As he remembers from the Limbo scene in which he says a Chinaman only talks, no fighting, he forsakes talking right away. This is the very concrete first step of action he takes after knowing who he is. He does not need to rely on mere talking.

62

His attention directed back to the documentary business, Tam is tempted to make a documentary in which Ovaltine's fake story of a self-made hero and a heroic father will be exposed nakedly. Tam vilely guarantees to Popcorn the documentary would be a good movie. He explains what he will do: "Make up some hokey connection between faking up a father, not knowing your past, and the killer instinct. But he's an old man now. Trusts me. I've failed all the old men that ever trusted me. Sold 'em out, watched 'em die, lost their names" (62). He also confesses, "My whiteness runneth over and blackness… but people still send me back to the kitchen" (63). In this elliptical way of self-confession, Tam also reveals his desperation to please whites, or the despair of not fulfilling his American dream—to be recognized and respected. But in a second, he changes his mind from muckraking Ovaltine's lies to making a straight documentary film. The crucial factor lies in Tom's remarks, "You're oversensitive. You can't be oversensitive." Tam agrees with his alter ego's diagnosis but he expresses his decision at once: "You're right. I can't be oversensitive. It's like havin too much taste. But that's me oversensitive. And I like it. I'm not going to dig up the Dancer. Mock his birth, make a fool of him just to make a name for myself. That's the way it is with us Chinaman cooks. Dat's the code of the kitchen, children" (63). Perhaps the change is too fast a turn that one might argue that it is not easy to spot Tam's newly acquired recognition and respect. However, this movie Tam will make, "a straight, professional, fight film," represents how Tam sees himself clearly, without self-loathing, guile, a mask, shame, or escape, but an honest one. He will face himself and the truth directly now.

This is the moment in which he finds his inner balance. This is also the moment when he manifests he is no more under the spell of Ovaltine and is disenchanted of his black idolatry due to Popcorn's honesty (D. Kim 196). Elaine

Kim is right to point out the play contains a series of lessons for Chinese Americans and that the most central of these is "that Asian American culture can be formed neither by imitating Whites nor by imitating Blacks" (186), but I disagree with her view that "instead of building a new manhood and a new culture […] through his imaginative writing, Chin creates an overriding sense of utter futility of the male protagonist's efforts to redefine himself" (186). If one reads the last part of the play closely, one would find a very different Tam. Besides his change in dropping mere talking and decision in making a straight documentary film, he begins to face his injured self and not to run away from the traumatic past. His direct confrontation with himself and his ensuing acts are definitely not signs of "futility." When Kenji asks him, "No hard feelings," Tam can proudly respond with a grin, "Damn straight I have hard feelings, And I like 'em, they're mine! Thank you" (63-64). Without any hypocritical pretense, this positive answer shows Tam's direct acceptance of truth.

Then he retreats to the kitchen to fry "chicken" for them. Tam takes up this cooking job, the job that is regarded with dishwashing as one fitting for women. But this womanizing job is subverted into a new job for someone who can take it straight without any gender or racial bias. This image of the Chinaman cook Tam presents himself in is a successful counter discourse of the effeminate Chinaman. Just like Popcorn's question, "What's wrong with a dishwasher?" There is nothing wrong with a cook. Hence, it is an outright subversion for Tam to be "the Chinaman cook" to fry "chicken," symbolizing he can reappropriate such a racist stereotype and empower the once denigrated image of the Chinaman. With the same attitude August Wilson also has in facing the distorted image and miserable past of his people, Frank Chin and Jefferey Paul Chan adopt the resistance discourse: "Us Chinamans mean to reverse the changes with our writing" (qtd.

Goshert 47). In John Charles Goshert's terms, Chin and Chan's "disruptive noise of resistance" dismantles the stereotypes that historically had marked the limit of expression for Asian American art (47). Insisting on using the same term, "Chinaman," Chin reverses the denigrating image into an image of self-esteemed; likewise, the image of the cook which Tam is attached to is also transformed strategically and symbolically. This is the rehabilitation and renewal one should learn from *The Chickcoop Chinaman.*

Moreover, toward the end of the play when Tam is delivering his closing monologue with the cook's apron on, he tells about the story of his grandmother's generation who sweated their whole life to build the railroad in the Sierra Nevada.

> My Grandmaw told me, children, [...] in the old West when Chinamans was the only electricity and all the thunder in the mountains [...] sometimes she heard a train. A Chinaman borne, high stepping Iron Moonhunter, liftin eagles with its breath. [...] The house she said was like when her father came back from the granite face and was put in the next room, broken and frostbit on every finger and toe of him and his ears and the nose, from the granite face [...] (65)

The Chinaman depicted in this Chinese American legend metamorphoses himself into the Iron Moonhunter, the train, which manifests the great contribution of these early Chinese railroad workers. Without the dedication of these Chinese American heroes chiseling out the granite in the mountains, America would not be America today. Therefore, his ode to those anonymous Chinese railroad workers connects the nameless "frontier" Chinese workers with numerous nameless early Chinese settlers like Tam's father in this play.[34] Thus, respect from within for

---

[34] Yu-cheng Li in his chapter on Chin's *Donald Duk* cites Boji Liu's account of Francis L. K. Hsu's account of how Chinese workers labored to help build the railroad, whose importance then was intentionally eliminated by whites. See Lee, pp. 119-20.

one's forebears and father can then be passed down to every Chinese American.

Dorothy R. McDonald analyzes Frank Chin's heroes and believes that, articulate as they are, they are "incapable of the action necessary to fulfill the hope and promise of the past" (xiv). However, in my opinion, Tam in *The Chickencoop Chinaman* not only takes the aforementioned action to manifest his recognition of his former biased ideology, but he also at the end of the play incorporates a very constructive image—Chinese railroad worker and the Iron Moonhunter—into the redefinition of a Chinaman. That is, Chinamen are active;[35] furthermore, they are indispensable to the development and prosperity of the American West. Many critics have applauded Chin's efforts in bringing to the foreground Chinese Americans' most vital contribution to the building of this nation by disclosing the Chinese railroad coolies' bitter life in building the transcontinental railroad (Sau-ling Wong, *Asian* 151; Li, "Formation" 216; D. Kim 199). Even if as Sau-ling Wong asserts after a fruitless search, "There seems to be a good possibility that Frank Chin invented the Iron Moonhunter legend" (*Asian* 226 footnote 34), this image of Chinese railroad workers, the Iron Moonhunter, should be deemed as an effective means of counter memory that Foucault has so inspiringly evoked in his writing. This brings to light "the history of racial marginalization to which Asian Americans have been subjected and record[s] those male heroic figures who were able to resist and transcend this marginalization" (D. Kim 197). Although, as Daniel Kim points out, Chin very possibly "ends up pretty much where he began: in thrall to an African American ideal of black identity" (199) by picking up the railroad imagery used by many

---

[35] As Viet Thanh Nguyen argues, "It is important to note that Chinese immigrants vigorously resisted, through legal means at the very least, the discrimination directed against them" (154). See Charles J. McClain, *In Search of Equality: The Chinese Struggle against Discrimination in Nineteenth-Century America* (1994) for further elaboration.

African Americans,[36] it is still very important for Chin to resort to "an affective counter-memory that not only discloses the removal of Chinese American history and their subservient position, but in the very process of disclosure negates the discursive oppression and constitutes the ethnic self as subject" (Li, "Formation" 216). This last speech of Tam's thus not only reclaims the nineteenth century but raises Chinese workers' importance. Furthermore, it is indicative of Tam's conviction of self-recognition and self-respect.

Cultural theorists Charles Taylor in his "The Politics of Recognition" and Jurgen Habermas in his "Struggles for Recognition in the Democratic Constitutional State" put an emphasis on the significance of mutual recognition for all ethnic groups, if peace and progress are to be found in a multicultural society (Gutmann 25-74; 107-48). Speaking generally about feminism, race relations, and multiculturalism, Taylor contends that "the withholding of recognition can be a form of oppression" (36) and he emphasizes that "we all *recognize* the equal value of different cultures; that we not only let them survive, but acknowledge their *worth*" (64). In a similar spirit, Habermas also speaks for respect in a multicultural society: "In multicultural societies the coexistence of forms of life with equal rights means ensuring every citizen the opportunity to grow up within the world of a cultural heritage and to have his or her children grow up in it without suffering discrimination because of it" (131-32). However, Habermas also points out that every culture has to find its strength for

---

[36] Although Daniel Y. Kim regards that Chin's embrace of the railroad imagery "seems to have been patterned after an African American 'original'" (199), I think Chin's intention to evoke Chinese railroad workers' bitter life and heroic past should not be overlooked. Whereas African American use of railroad imagery stresses the immense locomotive power of the train and its journey through the afflicted South, Chin's imagery of the Iron Moonhunter myth has a very close connection to the men who made the transcontinental railroad come true. Chin himself also once worked as a railway brakeman, "the first Chinese-American brakeman on the Southern Pacific Railroad, the first Chinaman to ride the engines" (qtd. in Goshert 45). It is thus important to note Chin's effort to put myth and history, synthesis and hybridity together.

regeneration. "Cultures survive only if they draw the strength to transform themselves from criticism and secession" (Habermas 132). Stuart Hall, Paul Gilroy, and many other theorists and critics all believe people of the ethnic cultures who once suffered from Euro-American subjugation have to confront their own history, to reconstruct their history and identity, and to rebuild their confidence. After all, without self-recognition and self respect, one cannot generate recognition and respect from others either.

IV. The Interethnic Solidarity

As the solidarity depicted in Wilson's *The Piano Lesson*, there is also a strong coalition in Chin's *The Chickencoop Chinaman*. While in the former Boy Willie and Berniece's cooperation to defeat the white subjugation is intraracial, the characters' help of each other in the latter is cross-racial. In the first place, Tam and Kenji's friendship reflects a strategic coalition between Chinese Americans and Japanese Americans. Social scientists who did research on "the Chinese and Japanese immigrants in the first half of the twentieth century emphasized ethnic solidarity or ethnic ties as an important aspect of Chinese and Japanese communities" (qtd. in Min 87). Ronald Takaki also points out among first-wave Chinese and Japanese immigrants ethnic solidarity was developed (473). Scholars like Yen Le Espirita have also termed the phenomenon like this "panethnicity" "to describe the political alliance between different Asian ethnic groups in the US that results in the formation of a political alliance called 'Asian America'" (qtd. In Nguyen 154 footnote 5). It is therefore easy to surmise that Tam and Kenji's long-term friendship originates from their united struggle against racial discrimination when in school.

Besides the alliance between Chinese American (Tam) and Japanese American (Kenji), the play features a very rare portrayal of interethnic solidarity between an Asian American and an African American. Sau-ling Wong has remarked on the rarity and uncommonality of an African American presence in Chinese American Literature and Studies ("Yellow and Black" 16).[37] As pointed out by Wong, many Chinese immigrants and Chinese American immigrant writers did not think highly of blacks ("Yellow and Black" 48); hence, it is very unusual to find solidarity between the yellow and the black in Chinese American Literature. As mentioned before, Chin himself and this kind of black idolatry are products of the Black Power Movement in the 1960s. Inspired and encouraged by African Americans' persistence, "in the late 1960s [...] a loosely organized social movement known as the Asian American movement arose to protest anti-Asian racism and exploitation" (Maeda 1081). Because both Asians and blacks shared a common oppression and because a coalition would provide an effective basis for resistance, panethnic solidarity consequently would be an ideal counter hegemonic strategy. This is also the background for Chin's proposition of interethnic solidarity.

Blacks occupy an important role in Tam and Kenji's mind and life. Although Kenji's identification with blacks and Tam's idolatry of Ovaltine and Charlie Popcorn are signs of escapism and substitution, Chin still presents his respect and admiration of blacks in the play through the black character—Charlie Popcorn. Through Popcorn's mouth, Tam learns that Ovaltine also lacks faith in his own past. "The revelation that Ovaltine's past is fictitious suggests Chin's ambivalence toward Asian American romantization of blackness" (Maeda

---

[37] Although Wong mentions Frank Chin's proposition to take blacks as a model, she does not include *The Chickencoop Chinaman* in her discussion. However, she analyzes two general features of African Americans in Chinese American Literature: "One family of the yellow and the black," and "different paths of the yellow and the black." More often than not, blacks are depicted negatively in Chinese American writings, which is what Wong means by "different paths of the yellow and the black." For more information, see Sau-ling Wong, "The Yellow and the Black: The African American Presence in Sinophone Chinese American Literature."

1097).[38] However, on Popcorn's back, when in a state of sleep dreaming after complete physical exhaustion, Tam recounts the failure of his marrying white and his divorce. "At his lowest point, weak and humiliated by a white woman, Tam relies on a black man to hold him up" (Maeda 1097-98). Admittedly, Chinese Americans like Tam owe the credit to blacks for their offering of themselves as inspiring counterparts and comrades. As Daryl J. Maeda asserts, "emulating blackness provided a way to recuperate Asian American masculinity" (1081). Popcorn's sharp words to ask Tam to get disenchanted of Ovaltine's fabricated masculine lineage, to recognize the true value of his father "Chinatown kid," and his assistance to physically carry him through "the Limbo" are all manifestations of Chinese and blacks' close connection and coalition to combat racist emasculation. This is the interethnic solidarity these ethnic people need.

In *Hegemony & Social Strategy*, Laclau and Mouffe particularly expand the base of the working class which Marxists used to fight for to incorporate more groups: "urban, ecological, anti-authoritarian, anti-institutional, feminist, anti-racist, ethnic, regional, or that of sexual minorities" (159), whose struggles have all been unsatisfactorily termed as "new social movements." Commenting on Laclau and Moffe's discourse, Jacob Torfing further explicates their concept by stating, "plural democracy, and the struggles for freedom and equality it engenders, should be deepened and extended to all areas of society" (256). Laclau and Mouffe believe no group can ignore other groups' struggles against antagonism of the privileged class. They particularly highlight the importance of alliance with other forces of anti-racism, anti-sexism, and anti-capitalism (141).

---

[38] This ambivalence might be why Josephine Lee thinks Chin's play "complicates the idea of Asian American maleness more than it resolves it" (88). Chin first allows the black boxer hero to wear an aura through Tam and Kenji's pious worship, then strips off blacks' glamorous by exposing their lack, and finally presents the protagonist's poignant self-awakening and self-esteem through a black mentor father figure.

Similarly, what Chin has made manifest in this play is the importance of such alliance across races; cooperation between Chinese Americans and Japanese Americans, and coalition between Asian Americans and African Americans are accentuated. Due to their common subjugated racial position, those marginalized should, like Laclau and Mouffe suggested, work together to resist white subjugation.

V. Conclusion

Different from the white American dream, the Chinese American dream depicted in Chin's *The Chickencoop Chinaman* focuses more on the moral imperative—to have equality, and, two more practical themes are added—recognition and respect. The protagonist Tam Lam used to see Chinese Americans, his father, and himself from a white perspective, but he is not aware that his perception is warped. Consequently, his identification is dangerous and denigrating. Chin shows us anyone of an ethnic group who would like to have a share in the pursuit of the American dream, like any other members in mainstream society, will have to first possess keen insights into the system of knowledge manipulated by white ideology. Without breaking through the imprisonment of the self-contemptuous images, history, and identity, one cannot truly embrace himself. Nor can he respect Chinese American history and people, let alone his father and himself. In other words, he will be farther and farther away from obtaining equality, tolerance, recognition, and respect from others.

Like Wilson's *The Piano Lesson*, *The Chickencoop Chinaman* also shows that the ethnic people who were once persecuted by whites need a counter strategy to rebuild themselves. They do not need to shy away from the denigrated image or past; instead, they should confront it, point out the significance of its distortion, and replace it with renewed meanings. In a nutshell, Chin in this play offers us an initiation quest in which the protagonist finally obtains knowledge and recognition of himself with the help of a black mentor. Through BlackJap Kenji's friendship and particularly Charlie Popcorn's teaching, Tam unlearns his father and his roots, and gains respect for other Chinese Americans, his father, and himself. With newly acquired recognition and respect, Tam, though he continues his roaming, can eliminate his American nightmare and proceed to realize his American dream.

Chapter Four

The American Dream for Chicano America

in Luis Valdez's *Zoot Suit*

I. Introduction

According to the American Census Bureau, Hispanic Americans have recently become the largest minority group in the United States, replacing African Americans. However, Hispanic Americans' socio-political status has not been improved with the rapid growth of their population. As Banks notes, "It is misleading to consider Hispanics one ethnic group. While the various Hispanic groups share a past influenced significantly by Spain and the Spanish language, there are tremendous historical, racial, and cultural differences between and within them" (317).The various names for Hispanic Americans reflect the complex diversity of their ethnic origins because they are from different places such as Mexico, Cuba, Puerto Rico, and Latin America. The plurality of ethnic constituency may be one of the reasons why it is harder for Hispanic Americans to produce counter discourses against whites' racial discrimination and subjugation.

According to the official definition, Hispanic is "one of several terms used to categorize persons whose ancestry hails either from Spain, the Spanish-speaking countries of Latin America, or the original settlers of the traditionally Spanish-held Southwestern United States. The term is used as a broad form of classification in the U.S. census, local and federal employment, and numerous business market researches."[39] Other terms related to Hispanic Americans include Mexican Americans, Chicanos/as, Mechicanos/as, and Latinos/as. [40] The Spanish-speaking feature allows many from diverse geographical origins to be qualified as Hispanic; however, this heterogeneity of Hispanic Americans leads to difficulties in producing a unified coalition.

About Chicano or Chicana

Today the majority of Hispanic Americans are composed of people who migrated from Mexico, and Mexican Americans are "both the largest and the fastest growing Hispanic group" (Banks 317). Historically, the term "Mexican" has had "so harshly pejorative a connotation" (Paredes 51) in the United States that many Mexican American writers wish to have a new way and term to represent themselves; then, according to Raymund A. Paredes, Mario Suarez in 1947 coined the term "Chicano," "simply the short way of saying *mexicano*" (56). Mexican Americans were in the land that is now the United States before the Anglo Americans came.[41] They became an ethnic minority when the United States occupied and finally took Mexico's northern territories in 1845. Although the Treaty of Guadalupe Hidalgo was supposed to protect the native Mexicans, "Mexican Americans were made second class citizens by Anglo-Americans who migrated and settled in the Southwest" (Banks 323). Ironically, due to the Anglo

---

[39] For the definition of Hispanic, see "Hispanic," http://en.wikipedia.org/wiki/Hispanic.

[40] According to Carl R. Shirley and Paula W. Shirley, Chicano is derived from Mexicano with the "x" pronounced as "ch" (5). The term "Mechicano" is invented by theatre scholar Jorge Huerta who coins it in his study of Mexican American drama in search of a national Chicano spirit (*Chicano Theatre* 8).

[41] Before 1168 these people's ancestors mostly inhabited the area from today's Texas to California. Some scholars believe the Chicanos/as descend historically from Indians (Arteaga 9). They had their first contact with the Europeans in 1519 when Hernan Cortes, the Spanish conquistador, and a group of Spaniards arrived in the region that is now Mexico. Other American groups who were in America before the Anglos' arrival include the American Indians, Aleuts, Eskimos, and Native Hawaiians.

oppression,[42] these people who used to reside in the Southwest are now landless and poverty-stricken. Moreover, the Mexican Revolution in 1910 also forced many Mexicans to migrate north seeking job opportunities. As Catherine Wiley states, these Chicanos' ancestors "left Mexican territory for many of the same reasons European and Asian immigrants left their nations of origins to provide a rich life for those to come" (99). Because of the Great Depression, thousands of Mexicans were "encouraged" or forced to go to Mexico without the benefits of legal proceedings, and again in 1954 because of "Operation Wetback" in response to the Bracero Program, several thousand Mexicans were deported without due legal process. These complicated historical and diasporic factors reveal why it has been difficult for Mexican Americans to achieve their American dream.

Mexican American playwright Luis Valdez saw the sadness of being Chicano/a in America; Valdez's plays and the stage productions of his theatrical troupe El Teatro Campesino never fail to explore the dire situation of this minority group. In his *Zoot Suit*, Valdez uses real historical events—the Sleepy Lagoon Murder Case and the Zoot Suit Riots—to bring to the foreground the adaptation of the first and second generations of Mexican Americans and their difficult positions of identity. In this chapter, I discuss the American dream for Chicano Americans presented in Valdez's *Zoot Suit*, and examine the effectiveness of Valdez's theatrical strategies in arousing Chicanos/as' reflection on and reaction against the hegemony of whites.

The Distorted Subjectivity

The Chicanos/as have suffered many injustices in America, but no other injustices could be as devastating as being regarded as barbarian or subhuman.

---

[42] For information regarding how Anglos stripped Mexicans of their land and the relevant oppression, see Raymund A. Paredes, "The Evolution of Chicano Literature."

This obnoxious and insulting denigration, however, truly existed in 1942, at the time when the historical Sleepy Lagoon Murder Case happened. We might find it hard to believe but a report written by Captain E. Duran Ayers, Chief of the Foreign Relations Bureau of the Los Angeles County Sheriff's Department, publicly indicates in a press release this kind of xenophobic and Eurocentric mindset when he announces:

> The biological basis is the main basis to work from. Although a wild cat and a domestic cat are of the same family, they have certain biological characteristics so different that while one may be domesticated, the other would have to be caged to be kept in captivity; and there is practically as much difference between the races of man as so aptly recognized by Rudyard Kipling when he said when writing of the Oriental. 'East is East and West is West and never the twain shall meet' which gives us an insight into the present problem because the Indian, from Alaska to Patagonia, is evidently Oriental in background—at least he shows many of the Oriental characteristics, especially so in his utter disregard for the value of life. (Morales and Sangrando 13)

Although Captain Ayer is talking about the Indians, he does not distinguish Amerindians from Mexican Americans. He identifies Indians with Orientals and in his opinion Amerindians, Mexicans and Orientals are all inferior to whites in their human capacity and he believes the biological difference is well justified. He then continues to discuss the bloody ritual of the Aztec to further show evidence of the inferiority of Amerindians. This debased identity of Hispanic Americans is obviously and intentionally distorted by a white law-enforcer.

In addition to the subhuman, or barbarian, identity, Chicanos/as are also stereotyped as passive. They are said to be "passive subjects who simply let history happen" (Broyles-Gonzalez 202), a "more or less voiceless, expressionless minority" (McWilliams 302). As fruit pickers or farmhands, many Mexicans do not have a legal residential status in America and their second-generation children born in America, though supposedly American citizens, are also given an unfair treatment. The pervading air in society, particularly in the pre-war era, was very hostile to Mexican Americans, who used to be regarded as passive, lascivious, and ignorant. However, as a contrast to their docile and meek image, they were also depicted as "treacherous and cruel" (Paredes 36). James A. Banks points out that the stereotypes, "which depicted the Mexican American as criminal and violent, were perpetuated by the established Anglo press, especially the Hearst newspaper" (333). In sum, this docile or barbarian stereotype has long been implanted in the minds of whites as well as Chicanos/as, which also has become a vicious circle. In other words, Mexican Americans, internalizing the distorted identity, have imposed upon themselves an inferior identity and have eventually become the distorted and stereotyped Chicanos/as. A critic poignantly points out that internal colonialism "keeps the Mechicano in his subservient place" (Huerta, *Chicano Theatre* 9).

Luis Valdez

Regarded as "the father of Chicano theatre" by scholars Nicolas Kanellos and Jorge Huerta (*Chicano Drama* 6), Luis Valdez has a grassroots background. Born to migrant farm workers in 1940, Valdez "periodically helped his family in the fields, as they moved from farm to farm, following the planting and harvest schedule" (Galens and Spampinato 269).[43] After graduating from San Jose State University with a Bachelor's degree in English, Valdez worked with the radical street theatre, the San Francisco Mime Troupe, for a year before helping Hispanic labor leader Cesar Chavez organize El Teatro Campesino in 1965. As Carl R.

---

[43] For further information about the life of Luis Valdez, see Kanellos's "Luis Miguel Valdez" in *Dictionary of Literary Biography*, and "Luis (Miguel) Valdez" in *Contemporary Author Online*.

Shirley and Paula W. Shirley assert, "All accounts of modern Chicano theatre begin with the year 1965, invoke the name of Luis Valdez and concentrate on the activities of El Teatro Compesino" (68). However, though still believing that "theatre should serve as an instrument of change in society" (Jimenez 118), Valdez has changed considerably his approach to theatre production and dramaturgy since his early work with El Teatro Campesino (Wattenberg 411), evolving from agitprops for Mexican farm workers to plays appealing to white, middle-class, mainstream viewers as well as to his traditional audience. *Zoot Suit* is one such example demonstrating his new strategy, and also probably "the Chicano play best known to Anglo audiences to date" (Shirley and Shirley 85). It had a tremendously successful run in California in 1978 and became the first Chicano play performed on a Broadway stage, in 1979.

The Historical Sleepy Lagoon Murder Case, the Zoot Suit Riots, and the Play

When conceiving *Zoot Suit*, Valdez thought it was time to reveal a period in their history that is generally neglected in the history books (Huerta, *Chicano Theatre* 179). He "drew directly from contemporary Angeleno newspapers and People v. Zammora and based many of the characters on real men and women" (C. Ramirez 19). Valdez in this play calls our attention to the "constructedness" of historical constructions of the past. In August 1942, a Mexican American youth called Henry Leyvas and 23 other young men of his "Zoot Suit" Gang were indicted for murdering another Mexican American young man Jose Diaz.[44] Henry Leyvas was beaten by his rival gang on the night of murder at the reservoir nicknamed "Sleepy Lagoon." When he returned armed with his men for the purpose of revenge, they were mistaken by the victim's family to be the rival gang

---

[44] For a detailed account of the Sleepy Lagoon Murder Case and the Zoot Suit Riots, see Mauricio Mazon, *The Zoot-Suit Riots: The Psychology of Symbolic Annihilation.*

who early on came to assault the family's birthday gathering. In their fight, Diaz was killed but no one saw clearly who killed him.

Of the twenty-four Chicano boys indicted, seventeen were convicted and were all sent to San Quentin Penitentiary. (Of the twenty-four, two boys who had enough money for their own lawyers demanded separate trials, and their cases were dismissed for insufficient evidence.) However, in October 1944, the District Court of Appeals reversed the convictions of all the defendants and the case was later dismissed due to lack of evidence.

When the murder case was reported in 1942, the newspapers intentionally manipulated the reportage to create a sensation; they played it up as a "Mexican crimewave." Soon in 1943, a clash occurred between Chicano young men and the servicemen in downtown Los Angeles. Many Chicanos were beaten and their zoot suits stripped off publicly by the white servicemen. This is the so-called Zoot Suit Riots. But the press once again presented a one-sided report and put the blame on the zooters and heralded the servicemen.

As professed at the onset of the play, Valdez mixes facts and fantasy in *Zoot Suit.* He follows the basic historical line, but he also makes some alterations of the facts, such as changing the name of the gang leader and adding one white female character. The play is divided into two acts with Act One centering on the ball, the fights, and the arrest. On the night before joining the army for World War II, Henry Reyna attends a ball with his girlfriend Della, his sister Lupe, his young brother Rudy, and his men of the 38th Street Gang. Rafas, the leader of their rival gang, the Downey Gang, is beaten and humiliated by Henry when he brings his girlfriend to the ball because Rafas tries to attack Rudy. Later Henry leaves the ball early with Della to go to Sleepy Lagoon, where he is beaten by Rafas and his gang for revenge. Nearby Sleepy Lagoon is a Mexican family having a big gathering but their happy celebration is ruined by Rafas's gang. So when Henry returns with his gang in search of the Downey Gang, he and his gang are met by the Mexican family who mistake them for the Downey Gang. In the dark and angry fight, Della seems to see an unknown man beating another man vehemently. When they are arrested for this man's murder, Lieutenant Edwards and Sergeant Smith treat them as base criminals and the press also uses a racist perspective to recount the murder case. The people's lawyer George Shearer defends the boys and a Jewish woman Alice Bloomfield also helps organize a committee on the defendants' behalf to help with their appeal. However, the racist Judge F. W. Charles and the racist jury find the boys guilty and send them to jail.

Act Two depicts the prison life of Henry and his gang members, Henry's release, and the celebration of his release. Henry first distrusts his white lawyer George Shearer and human right activist Alice Bloomfield, but he finally has faith in them. Though both try hard not to get involved emotionally, Alice and Henry develop a relationship, especially after Henry is set up to be in solitary by the prison guard. Finally they win the murder case appeal and are released. At home, Henry has to decide to choose between Della and Alice, and to choose between being an assimilationist or a defiant pachuco.

In order to further depict Henry's mentality and the Chicano spirit, Valdez creates on the stage El Pachuco, Henry's alter ego, to be the narrator for the entire play. He is a bridge between the audience and Henry. At one time, he also roleplays Henry's brother Rudy when Rudy's zoot suit is stripped off in the Zoot Suit Riots. The play ends in several versions of the life of Henry Reyna, which the playwright intentionally sets up for the readers and spectators to think more about.

After *Zoot Suit* was first performed in 1978, "the audience loved the production" (Huerta, *Chicano Theatre* 181), and "was undaunted in their enthusiastic response to the production" (Huerta, *Chicano Theatre* 177). It received criticism from both positive and negative extremes. Some critics, particularly such Hispanic critics like Yolanda Broyles-Gonzalez (20), Jorge Huerta (*Chicano Theatre* 22-23), and Elizabeth Ramirez (195), praise the play for the success of its theme, mixed form of realism, expressionism, and epic theatre, and they hail the significance of drawing so many Hispanics into theatres and reaching Broadway. The Press even calls the box office success a new "Zoot Suit Riot" (Huerta, "*Zoot Suit*"). This phenomenon is regarded as a Chicano Movement of the 1970s, and a symbol of cultural nationalism. One critic praises the play's close connection with the community (Kanello 7). Others champion its achievement into the white establishment theatre.

While some critics (Babcock 1995; Davy 2003; Huerta 1982, 1992, 1993) hail the success of the historical significance of this play, white reviewers like R. G. Davis and Betty Diamond, and Richard Eder criticize the poverty of the political and aesthetic quality. Davis and Diamond and Eder,[45] simply discredit its political and aesthetic effect, claiming it a "poorly written play." These caustic critics happened to be the white play reviewers who held great power in swaying the New York audience.[46] Therefore, the Broadway waterloo is inevitable (Davis and Diamond 6). The play may not be as good as Eugene O'Neill's *Long Day's Journey into Night*, but the fastidious white reviewers' comments remind one of the racist law enforcers in the play. One critic calls such harsh reception from the

---

[45] Critic Daniel Davy think these critiques have overlooked a critically significant aspect of the play—"the creation of a communal protagonist in the play" (73). For a discussion on the negative reviews and criticism on *Zoot Suit*, see Daniel Davy's "The Enigmatic God: Mask and Myth in *Zoot Suit*," pp. 71-73, and Broyles-Gonzalez pp. 190-95.

[46] Yolanda Broyles-Gonzalez analyzes the scathing reviews of the Broadway production and says, "Various New York critics resented the very subject matter of *Zoot Suit* because of the guilt it evidently made them feel" (190).

white play reviewers "white man's arrogance" (Kanello 10), which in a sense parallels the biased and racist press and law enforcers Valdez aims to attack in the play. In addition to negative criticism spiced with white aesthetic judgment, some female critics such as Yolanda Broyles-Gonzalez condemn the downplaying of the importance of Chicana characters in the play and criticize Valdez's condescending attitude to please white society by adding a white female protagonist to this play. Few of the critics notice the playwright's intention to reveal the distorted and framed identity whites would like the Chicanos/as to have. Almost none of them discuss the playwright's proposal for the Hispanic Americans to work with other marginalized groups.

In this chapter, I would like to argue that Valdez uncovers the white institutionalization at work in the Sleepy Lagoon Murder Case and the Zoot Suit Riots. These kinds of white hegemonic institutions are merely the American nightmares to Chicano Americans. Valdez actually dissects the passive, tamed, and distorted identity whites impose on the Chicanos/as, and encourages them to embrace an active and independent Chicano/a identity in cooperation with other support groups and oppressed minority groups if Chicano Americans would like to realize their American dream. Hence, unlike Wilson's device to include black characters as foils to manifest a wrongly conceived American dream influenced by whites, and unlike Chin's arrangement to present the internalized distorted subjectivity of Chinese Americans, Valdez attacks whites head-on, exposing their distortion of Chicanos/as. Wilson rarely includes white characters in his plays; Chin also has only one imaginary white character in his play; however, Valdez directly presents the whites on stage because the white hegemonic institutionalization is the source of the American nightmares to Chicanos/as.

II. Chicanos' American Nightmare: White Distortion

Luis Valdez started his playwriting career tightly with *la raza*, the people. However, he later left the Union so as to further develop his art and to spread his works to a wider audience.[47] Since Valdez is from a farm laborer's family, he knows with great familiarity about poverty and injustice of the Mexican American life. He sees clearly that Chicanos/as have suffered immensely not only physically but also mentally in this Anglo-dominated society. In order to manifest the distorted identity for and of Chicanos/as, Valdez resorts to the strategy of blending historical facts and fantasy to analyze the power dynamic at work in white hegemonic institutionalization. Probing into the mentality behind the white distortion, he finds whites give Chicanos/as a distorted identity so that this ethnic group will remain passive, silenced, and obedient.

Louis Althusser has told us, every State Apparatus controls its people through both the Repressive State Apparatuses (RSAs) and Ideological State Apparatuses (ISAs). When he discusses RSAs, he uses the army and the police as examples (145). In *Zoot Suit*, we see how the police and the prison guard and the Judge repress Henry and his men. Althusser continues to explain, "the Ideological State Apparatuses function massively and predominantly by ideology, but they also function secondarily by repression, even if ultimately, but only ultimately, this is very attenuated and concealed, even symbolic" (145). In addition to schools and churches, he also draws censorship as cultural ISA. In the play we find the ISA is embodied in the press.

Just like Michel Foucault's idea of panoptic surveillance, whites control the behavior, the language, and, more importantly, the thinking of Chicanos/as by

---

[47] For a more detailed account of Valdez's writing career, please see Martinez and Lomeli's *Chicano Literature: A Reference Guide*, pp. 399-403, and Jorge Huerta's *Chicano Theater: Themes and Forms* and his various articles on Valdez, or Nicholas Kanellos's "Luis Miguel Valdez," http://www.lrc.html.

means of laws, education, media, and ideology. In his study of panopticism, Foucault points out, all "the disciplines are techniques for assuring the ordering of human multiplicities" (*Discipline* 218). As one critic points out, Valdez's intention is to interrogate "the multitude of panoptic strategies exercised by the press and the courts; these strategies distort the cultural image of the Pachuco, purposefully misrepresenting it in order to exacerbate existing racial tensions (the historical criminalization of the zoot suit apparel is but one sign of this effort)" (Gutierrez-Jones 71). In the play, the white hegemonic institutionalization is represented by the press and the three law enforcers—the police, the prison guard, and the judge. When they deal with the Hispanic community, represented in the play by the zooters, they are likely to wear a racist lens. While the press hunts the zooters as if they were born debased criminals, the three agents of law enforcement further convict them as a diabolic enemy and scum to be eliminated.

A. The Distortion Manipulated by the Press

Valdez relentlessly attacks the complicity of the press with the law enforcers in distorting facts and in oppressing Chicanos/as. In Act One Scene Two "Mass Arrests" the Press and a Cub Reporter come with the police led by Lieutenant Edwards and Sergeant Smith to arrest Henry Reyna. "It was a Valdezian indictment of the press, which had helped create and perpetuate the racist hysteria of the period" (Huerta, *Chicano Theatre* 179). Although the Press represents several different newspapers, they all view the event from the same racist perspective. At the command of Lieutenant Edwards the pachucos spread for police photographs. Valdez ingenuously makes the Press serve as the police photographer shooting pictures for filing suspects. Meanwhile, the Press is announcing news headlines. It is of great importance for the Press to assume two roles here, purporting to the joint forces of the police and the press.

([...] The sirens fade and give way to the sound of a teletype. The
PACHUCOS *turn and form a lineup, and the* PRESS *starts shooting*
pictures as HE *speaks.*)
PRESS: The City of the Angels, Monday, August 2, 1942. The Los
Angeles Examiner, Headline:
THE LINEUP: (*In Chorus.*) Death Awakens Sleepy Lagoon (*Breath.*)
LA Shaken by Lurid "Kid" Murder.
PRESS: The City of the Angels, Monday, August 2, 1942. The Los
Angeles Times Headline:
THE LINEUP: One Killed, Ten Hurt in Boy Wars: (*Breath.*)
Mexican Boy Gangs Operating Within City.[48] (28)

Since it is America during war time, it is natural for American society to be highly

sensitive to disorder at home. However, the reaction toward this murder case is

excessively tainted with racial discrimination. The diction used in the four major

LA Newspapers (The Los Angeles Examiner, The Los Angeles Times, Los

Angeles Herald Express, and The Los Angeles Daily News) implies a desperate,

urgent crisis, especially when phrases like "'Kid' Murder," "Boy Wars,"

"Mexican Youths," "Boy Gangs," seem to endanger the "City of Angels," a

peaceful white paradise. In other words, the profit-oriented press, with the aim of

catching the readers' attention, brutally exploits and sacrifices the young

Chicanos/as for a piece of sensational news. As Henry expresses his view of the

futile appeal, he explains to George, "The press has already tried and convicted us.

Think you can change that?" (42). This explains why one critic would describe

the press as "villainous" (Broyles-Gonzalez 182), hinting at the Press as the

villain. Moreover, the antagonism between whites and Chicanos/as is whetted by

the long suppressed discontent with the pachuco and the so-called "war-time

hysteria." Hence, the confluence of oppressive forces soon ignites an incident like

---

[48] *Zoot Suit and Other Plays* (Houston: U of Houston, 1992), p. 28. All subsequent
references will be noted parenthetically in the text.

the Zoot Suit Riots between the two racial groups. It was true that "The Press succeeded in alarming the public and in stirring up anti-Mexican feelings" (Banks 334) because soon "hundreds of Anglos went into street" and they "began a massive attack on Mexican American youths. Many "zoot-suitors" were beaten and stripped naked in the streets" (Banks 334).

In Act One Scene 5 entitled "The Press" the police and the press (now consisting of the PRESS, the Cub Reporter, and a Newsboy) present their press conference with questions and answers on the basis of distorting and denigrating the pachucos. To coax people to buy newspapers, the press and the newsboy cry out, "Mexican Crime Wave Engulfs L.A." (38). (To echo in rhyme and derision, Lieutenant Edwards adds, "Slums breed crimes, fellas. That's your story.") Newsboy continues to shout with the racist language, "Zoot-suited Goons of Sleepy Lagoon!" and "The Mexican Baby Gangsters," making their profit opportunistically out of the exploitation and distortion of the Chicanos/as. As one critic puts it, "Newspapers are an insistent motif, reflecting the play's denunciation of the press role in whipping up anti-Hispanic sentiments" (Eder 13).

The Press not only deems Chicanos/as as low and base like animals but also thinks them foolish to want to be like whites. In Act Two Scene Six "Zoot Suit Riots" where a fight breaks out in a ballroom between zoot suiters led by Rudy and the servicemen composed of three sailors and a marine, the Press comes to cover the report of the riot live on air. Valdez skillfully and expressionistically replaces El Pachuco for besieged Rudy when he is about to be stripped of his zoot suit. The playwright makes it clear that the Press symbolizes both the biased media and the xenophobic American sentiments when the Press joins the servicemen to jeer, provoke, and overpower El Pachuco.

Far from presenting the event neutrally, the biased media, now a radio broadcast played by the Press, distorts the fact of the riot. In fact, it was the sailors at the ballroom who started the fight with Rudy by mistaking Bertha and Lupe for prostitutes. However, the Press reports, "Serious rioting broke out here today as flying squadrons of Marines and soldiers joined the Navy in a new assault on zooter-infested districts" (78). The apparent binary opposition between the good soldiers and the bad zooters is directly established in the strong phrase "zooter-infested districts" since the verb "infest" spontaneously conjures up pests or undesirables. By the same token, zooters, or Chicanos/as, are depicted as lower-class humans, or subhumans.

In the ensuing hot and provocative verbal confrontation, sailors, Bosun's Mate, Marine, and the Press jeer at El Pachuco's dress ("chango monkey suit"), cowardice ("[no] balls in them funny pants"), and their debased identity ("half monkey," "savages") (79-80). When the Pachuco tries to criticize how the Press and Anglos misunderstand the word "zoot," the Press does not hesitate to confess his discrimination. He claims, "You are trying to outdo the white man in exaggerated white man's clothes" (80). "You savages," continues the Press haughtily, "weren't even wearing clothes when the white man pulled you out of the jungle" (80). The Press's insult implies a twofold meaning. Firstly, like Fanon's and Said's interpreting colonizers framing up the colonized as their inferior other, whites also deem Chicanos/as, or Amerindians, as savages. Drawing examples from Western literature and academic scholarship, Said criticizes the anthropocentrism and Europocentrism of the westerners: "a white middle-class Westerner believes it his human prerogative not only to manage the nonwhite world but also to own it, just because by definition 'it [the Oriental]' is not quite as human as 'we' are" (108). The scholars of the West "formed a simulacrum of the Orient and reproduced it materially in the West, for the West" (Said 166). Like whites demonizing Orientals in Said's analysis, Anglos in America also regard and make non-Anglos, Chicanos/as here, the inferior other. The haughty subjugator even feels justified to redeem and subjugate the "savage."

Secondly, deep down in the colonizer's victorious pride lurks a strong fear of whites being defeated by the colonized when the colonized learn to mimic as well as outshine the colonizer. Homi Bhabha's theory of mimicry serves right here for us to understand why the colonizer has to oppress, suppress, or even terminate the existence of the colonized when the former is menaced by the latter. According to Bhabha, "Mimicry is, thus the sign of a double articulation; a complex strategy of reform, regulation and discipline, which 'appropriates' the Other as it visualizes power. Mimicry is also the sign of the inappropriate, however, a difference or recalcitrance which coheres the dominant strategic function of colonial power, intensifies surveillance, and poses an immanent threat to both 'normalized' knowledges and disciplinary powers" (86). This mimicry theory illustrates well why whites—sailors, Bosun's Mate, Marine, and the Press—have to strip off El Pachuco's zoot suit because "mimicry is at once resemblance and menace" (Bhabha 86). It is only through this indispensable humiliation and discipline, which is to strip off the mimic man's gimmick to outdo his master, that the subjugator can maintain his hegemonic stance.

B. The Distortion of the Law Enforcers

In addition to the biased press, the racist law enforcers are also scrutinized in the power dynamic of this iniquitous historical incident. It is not difficult for one to detect that the deeply rooted abhorrence of Chicanos/as from the three agents—the police, the prison guard, and the judge—stems from their unconscious racism. Both policemen Lieutenant Edwards and Sergeant Smith think Chicanos/as prone to commit crimes. While Lieutenant Edwards still wants to bargain with Henry to get the truth of the murder case, Sergeant Smith treats Chicanos/as as incorrigible and vile subhumans, just like Caliban in Shakespeare's *Tempest*. During the interrogation in Act One Scene Four, Lieutenant Edwards wants to get Henry sworn in the Navy if he discloses the truth about the murder case. But Sergeant Smith persuades his superior not to do so saying, "Forget it, Lieutenant. You can't treat these animals like people" (32). When he is left alone with Henry, he soon pompously attacks Henry's zoot suit, jeering, "I hear tell you pachucos wear these monkey suits as a kind of armor." He immediately resorts to a brutal way to extort and discipline his handcuffed suspect by beating him with a rubber sap until Henry passes out and falls to the floor. As racist as the police, the prison guard also calls Henry and his men "greaseball" and "bastard" (76) and he intentionally provokes Henry so that the Chicano is punished by being put in solitary confinement for his attack of the guard, i.e., for his contempt for the rule, and the white law.

Even more racist and pompous than the previous policemen and prison guard is Judge F. W. Charles, who practically holds more substantial legal and penal power in his hands. His distortion of Chicanos/as and his biased treatment of the suspects for the legal case are diabolic. Indeed, his racist thinking and behavior are so much in line with those of Lieutenant Edwards's that one cannot miss the hidden agenda when Valdez makes the same actor roleplay both Lieutenant Edwards, Judge Charles, and the Jury. (It so happens that another actor roleplays both the Press and the Prosecution.) These whites are equally the same in their racism. When the pachucos' white lawyer George demands an explanation why his defendants have been denied clean clothes and haircuts for three months, the Prosecution and Judge Charles offer seemingly justified but actually racist

90

reasons.

> PRESS: (*Jumping in.*) Your Honor, there is testimony we expect to develop that the 38th Street Gang are characterized by their style of haircuts...
> GEORGE: Three months, Your Honor.
> PRESS:...the thick heavy heads of hair, the ducktail comb, the pachuco pants...
> GEORGE: Your Honor, I can only infer that the Prosecution...is trying to make these boys look disreputable, like mobsters.
> PRESS: Their appearance is distinctive, Your Honor. Essential to the case.
> GEORGE: You are trying to exploit the fact that these boys look foreign in appearance! Yet clothes like these are being worn by kids all over America.
> PRESS: Your Honor...
> JUDGE: (*Bangs the gavel.*) I don't believe we will have any difficulty if their clothing becomes dirty.
> GEORGE: What about the haircuts, Your Honor?
> JUDGE: (*Ruling.*) The zoot haircuts will be retained throughout the trial for purposes of identification of defendants by witnesses. (52-53)

It is obvious Judge Charles, sacrificing the basic rights of Chicano/a youths, aims at making these defendants more detestable with their sloppy, dirty, and criminal-like appearance. An experienced Superior Court judge like him, Judge Charles tramples these youths' dignity with law. Moreover, he is bent on abusing their basic human rights at court by making "the defendants stand each time their names are mentioned" simply because "the Jury is having trouble telling one boy from another" (53). In spite of George's objection on the grounds of possible self-incrimination of the defendants when the Prosecution makes an accusation, the racist Judge does not budge.

Another example to illustrate Judge Charles's racial discrimination in disguise of law is his objection to George's request to have his defendants sit with him during the trial so that he might consult with them. Judge Charles answers, "No. This is a small courtroom, Mr. Shearer. We can't have twenty-two defendants all over the place" (53). When George cites support from the Federal and State constitutions, Judge Charles simply flouts, "Well, that is your opinion" (54). Judge Charles does not hesitate to hide his racism at all, even if he has to ignore or misinterpret the U.S. Constitution. He is so blinded by his racism that he is determined to nail these Chicanos to death.

It is no surprise when it comes to "The Conclusion of the Trial" Scene, the defendants are found guilty. The Jury is convinced by the white Prosecution (the Press) when he, in his concluding statement, employs emotional appeal, alerting them by saying, "The city of Los Angeles is caught in the midst of the biggest, most terrifying crime wave in its history. A crime wave that threatens to engulf the very foundations of our civic well-being" (61). He blatantly announces, "The specific details of this murder are irrelevant before the overwhelming danger of the pachuco in our midst. I ask you to find these zoot-suited gangsters guilty of murder and to put them in the gas chamber where they belong" (62). He evades the lack of evidence but keeps threatening the Jury whose life is supposed to be in danger. George also makes an effective concluding statement to appeal to the Jury's rational and moral capacity but to no avail. However, his argument happens to offer the best footnote to the Jury's conclusion of finding the boys guilty. Put in George's own words, the Jury's and the Judge's verdict demonstrate "racial intolerance and totalitarian injustice" and they are murdering "the spirit of racial justice in America" (62). But they don't care because they believe in that distorted Chicano identity, ignoring the fact and the truth. As Elizabeth Jacobs contends, the actions of the court consist of an all-white jury, a white prosecution lawyer, and a white judge, "mirror the events of the zoot suit riots themselves, when the *pachucos* were similarly demonized and 'symbolically annihilated, castrated, transformed" (85).

III. The Way to the American Dream: A New Chicano Identity

Even though the press and law enforcers impose the distorted racist identity on Hispanic Americans and cause them to have nightmares, Valdez has a clear message for his people through Henry Reyna. Instead of accepting the silenced, passive, and unworthy identity of Chicanos/as forced upon them by whites, Chicanos/as should have their own true identity that is indigenous, active, and dutiful if they want to improve their lives and realize their American dream. Moreover, another important message Valdez would like to convey is that Chicanos/as should cooperate with other support or marginalized groups. Through the three different facades of Henry's life—El Pachuco, the calm man, and the family man, we will find the identity of a Chicano should be indigenous, active, and dutiful, ready for coalition with others for survival and betterment.

A. The Indigenous Identity—El Pachuco

In *Zoot Suit*, the protagonist is comprised of Henry the man and El Pachuco. With this expressionistic device to dramatize Henry's split consciousness, the audience can read Henry's internal activities more clearly. El Pachuco can be regarded as an ambivalent characterization, with the negative drive and the dynamic, indigenous drive. Although Valdez wants El Pachuco to be of mythic indigenous origin, one should be aware that another side of El Pachuco is the negative character which Henry needs to learn to fight against. Apparently, El Pachuco serves as Henry's alter ego. Valdez himself explains in an interview, "The Pachuco is the Jungian self-image, the superego if you will" (Savran 265). The Pachuco also appears to be negative, pessimistic, and sardonic. As Huerta notices, " El Puchuco is Henry Reyna's alter ego, his pachuco-half that sometimes keeps him from doing things he otherwise would, such as saying 'thank you' to his lawyer" (*Chicano Theatre* 180). He may be just another voice inside Henry, dialogizing with the calm man, but he often chills Henry. For example, he tells Henry not to nurture hope for their appeal in Act Two Scene Three (73). Also, when Henry in Act Two Scene Five (78) is left alone in solitary, he entertains Henry with no hope for his appeal or release from his imprisonment. His bitter pessimism incurs Henry's antagonism and anger, so he is ordered by Henry to leave. El Pachuco does leave him and does not return until Henry is set free at the end of the play. El Pachuco's disappearance on stage in this period can be viewed symbolically as Henry's successful attempt to discipline his negative inclination.

The more significant function of El Pachuco, however, is his "unique" indigenousness. Many characteristics can be credited to the myth of El Pachuco, but in the play defiance is El Pachuco's champion. He is defiant in his difference. His dressing style endorses his uniqueness. Furthermore, Valdez would like to connect with emphasis El Pachuco and the Aztec myth to inform and instruct his Hispanic and non-Hispanic spectators that their priceless indigenous origin is also what they need to rebuild their subjectivity with. Although some critics dislike this pachuco emblem saying it is another barrio type, most critics think the pachuco refers to rebel, hero, and savior (Huerta, *Chicano Theatre* 4; C. Ramirez 2; Banks 337; Jacobs 83). I, however, want to particularly stress the indigenous and the different feature of the pachuco figure. Valdez's reinterpretation of the pachuco stereotype is a successful "iconoclasm." Critic Granger Babcock also applauds Valdez's strategy of revitalizing "outlaw" figures and he claims the playwright and other workers gave these stereotypes which were primarily the projections of Anglo-American fear and racism "a positive value" (217). "El Pachuco," claims Broyles-Gonzalez, "was rehabilitated during the Chicano movement and had been reconstituted as something of a positive antihero" (188).

At the inception of the play, El Pachuco emerges on stage by ripping open the

giant facsimile of a newspaper serving as the drop curtain, symbolizing this

Pachuco's breakthrough of the conventional stereotype. He, "proudly, slovenly,

defiantly makes his way downstage" and addresses the audience first in Spanish

then in English:

> Pachuco: [...]
> The Pachuco Style was an act in Life
> and his language a new creation.
> [...]
> A mythical, quizzical, frightening being
> precursor of revolution
> Or a piteous, hideous heroic joke
> deserving of absolution?
> I speak as an actor on the stage.
> The Pachuco was existential
> for he was an Actor in the streets
> both profane and reverential.
> It was the secret fantasy of every bato
> in or out of the Chicanada
> to put on a Zoot Suit and play the Myth
> mas chucote que la chingada. (25-26)

Valdez conveys to the audience that this figure of El Pachuco is a hybrid of

ambivalence—old and new materials, heroic and hideous spirits, and profane and

reverential airs. Through this once popular product of youth subculture, the

playwright reinterprets this "mythical, quizzical, frightening being."

The different feature of El Pachuco is highlighted by his mythic aura,

especially when he is stripped of his zoot suit in Act Two Scene Six "Zoot Suit

Riots." The playwright intentionally wants the audience to perceive that the

essence of a Chicano/a is indigenously Indian, or Aztec. In the stage direction, he

describes the stripping scene:

SWABBIE: You trying to outdo the white man in them glad rags, Mex? (*They fight now to the finish. EL PACHUCO is overpowered and stripped as HENRY watches helplessly from his position. The PRESS and SERVICEMEN exit with pieces of EL PACHUCO's zoot suit. EL PACHUCO stands. The only item of clothing on his body is a small loincloth. HE turns and looks at HENRY, with mystic intensity. HE opens his arms as an Aztec conch blows, and HE slowly exits backward with powerful calm into the shadows. HENRY comes downstage. HE absorbs the impact of what HE has seen and falls to his knees at the center stage, spent and exhausted. Lights down.*) (81)

The picture Valdez aims to invoke is the Aztec god—Quetzalcoatl, the feathered serpent (Savran 265). Stripped of its external "drapes," the Chicano is in fact the beautiful Indian god, with no humiliation or inferior demeanor.

While whites regard the racial difference of Chicanos/as as savage, Valdez sees the uniqueness and indigenity in their physiognomy and culture. Seeing the same unique display in these pachucos' zoot suits, the playwright likens the two in their difference and defiance. Critics also say he is the symbol of defiance (Huerta, *Chicano Theatre* 23; C. Ramirez 83). The zoot suit[49] speaks symbolically because clothes are a cultural difference (Gutierez-Jones 71). When Holly Alford discusses the origin of zoot suits, she states two important things: "first, mainly Mexican-Americans wore the suit in the western part of the United States and mainly African-Americans in the eastern part of the United states; second, most of these young men were socially and culturally disadvantaged, trying to let people know who they were through their clothing" (228). The typically exaggerated clothing, the badge of the pachuco, includes high waisted baggy pants,

[49] According to a fashion expert, "Zoot, as a verb, means something done or worn in an exaggerated style, but as a noun it is the ultimate in clothes" (Alford 226)

square-shouldered, oversized jacket long dangling key chain (Alford 225-26, 228).
These pachucos show their defiance and subversion not only in their dress but
also in language, which is a mixture of English, Spanish, and *calo*, as their
language.[50] As Kelly explains, "The language and culture of zoot suitors
represented a subversive refusal to be subservient" (qtd. C. Ramirez 2). Hence, El
Pachuco's way is to take pride in the Chicano's indigenous difference. Chicanos
should not conform to the whites' way and they, like those zooters, should resist
and deny the distorted images whites have imposed on them. Instead of feeling
ashamed of themselves, they should celebrate their indigenity and their
uniqueness.

B. The Active Identity

Henry, a man of different facades, has many consciousnesses functioning
simultaneously. Among them, El Pachuco's negative taunts often surface first
when challenges confront Henry. However, he gradually learns that observing
coolly and calculating well should precede his action. He forsakes El Pachuco's
self abandonment to hopelessness and passivity; he begins to trust those Anglos
who are willing to help. He becomes a man of action, not the man of quick
impetuous reaction like the old Henry beating his rival gang leader Rafas, but the
man of action after careful deliberation, especially when he is trapped beyond
hope. When Henry and his boys are detained before the trial, the white lawyer
George Shearer comes to take care of their case. Henry eyes this white lawyer
with suspicion and distrusts this gringo. George alerts them with the urgency and
criticality of this mass trial, advising them to do away with their petty nationalistic
concern. He argues,

---

[50] "*Calo*" is pachuco slang (C. Rameriz 2). The Chicano theatre is noted for its hybrid use
of language, or the "Spanglish." "Words and phrases in the two languages are constantly
interchanged depending upon the context" (Woodyard 95).

[…] The problem seems to be that I look like an Anglo to you. What if I were to tell you that I had Spanish blood in my veins? That my roots go back to Spain, just like yours? What if I'm an Arab? What if I'm a Jew? What difference does it make? The question is will you let me help you? (43)

What George has pointed out is whether Henry and his boys will trust him whatever his ethnic background might be. After some careful thinking, Henry then agrees to let George take care of their case. It is crucial here for Henry to learn to avoid stubborn self-evasiveness or not to reject others' help out of ignorance and arrogance. Under further consideration, he learns it might be wise to accept help.

Alice Bloomfield, the one organizing a citizens' "Sleepy Lagoon Defense Committee" (67) on the defendants' behalf, spares no effort in helping them. Ignoring her voluntarism and enthusiasm, Henry first rejects her help, which tremendously surprises and dismays her. When she begs him not to drop out of the appeal and to think about George and all the people that have contributed their time and money to the case, Henry simply bursts out refuting,

Why didn't you ask me? You think you can just move in and defend anybody you feel like? When did I ever ask you to start a defense committee for? Or a newspaper? Or a fundraising drive and all that other shit? I don't need defending, esa. I can take care of myself. (71)

The obstinate self indulgence stems from his sense of insecurity and self-abandonment. When Henry, explaining his suspicion, says to Alice, "You're just using Mexicans to play politics" (71), he seems to be demonstrating more of the pessimistic and distrustful El Pachuco part more. Thanks to Alice's outburst of rage inflicted by such unjust treatment, Henry finally learns to think and accept Alice, or others, as their comrade(s).

At the end of the play, Henry wavers between two fates: to continue his zoot suit outfit scorned by whites to manifest defiantly his uniqueness of being a Chicano, or to forsake his zoot suit and be like his father, an assimilated Mexican working quietly and diligently at the bottom of the social strata. Critic Huerta thinks this open ending with many possibilities suggests that Henry's future is not very bright (*Chicano Theatre* 184). However, remembering the Chicano Movement in the 1960s and 1970s in which many Mexican American workers aggressively opposed their conditions and organized unions and strikes, thus shattering the myth that Mexican Americans are docile workers, the playwright in the end of the play would galvanize his audience to take the same action, simply not to let the chance slip away. Hence, Valdez does not provide the audience with a definite final answer at the end of the play, for the purpose of giving his audience a chance to judge on their own. It matters less how Henry will end his life; after all, Henry has learned to be an active man with self-control. What matters more here is whether the audience can learn to take action. Thus, in my opinion, this open ending is an effective way to make the audience think and take action, too. This reader-response way to interpret the ending corresponds to Valdez's urge for his spectators to be active.

C. The Dutiful Identity

Besides the mythical Amerindian indigenous identity and the active identity, Valdez still retains the familiar but important good old Mexican strength for the new Chicano identity—the dutiful identity. One trait that distinguishes the Chicanos/as from some other American racial groups is that they stick to their family and they have a strong sense of family obligation. For Valdez, the family is the hope for future (Huerta, *Chicano Theatre* 10). Henry takes care of his brother and sister; in fact, he goes to jail to cover up for his younger brother in the murder case. He respects and loves his parents; moreover, he even decides to join the Navy to satisfy his father's wish to have his son as a "truly" assimilated American. Besides his family, he takes good care of his 38th Street Gang. It is this strong sense of family ties and brotherhood obligations that brings to the foreground the immense humanitarian capacity of this pachuco. Critic Elizabeth Ramirez also states, "Henry places the needs of his family and friends above his own, overcomes all obstacles, emerging as a defiant victor" (199). All this only shows that Chicanos/as are not "brown animals" as jeered at by whites; they are great dignified family men.

The dutiful magnitude is exemplified by two acts Henry does; one is the decision to go to jail to cover for his brother, as mentioned before; the other is his decision to take Della for his wife but not Alice at the end of the play. After the long fight against injustice, Henry and Alice develop a comradeship and love out of mutual understanding and steadfast support. However, Henry's girlfriend, whom he intended to marry before the murder case occurred, has also been involved in the murder case and has spent one year in prison and another year with Henry's parents after she has been expelled by her father. Henry finally decides to choose Della, but also with the thoughtful understanding of Alice.

The playwright's call to the dutiful aspect is reinforced at the end of the play when they win the appeal and return home. In Act Two Scene Nine "Return to the Barrio," Henry is surrounded by his family. His father, his mother, his wife-to-be, and his lover Alice all remind him of his family obligations. His lover Alice says to him, "You're home now, with your family, that's what matters" (91). His mother, comforting his uneasiness, tells him everything is going to be fine and advises him to "Marry Della and fill this house with children." However, she adds, "Just do one thing for me—forget the zoot suit clothes" (91). His father also says, "If there's one thing that will keep a man off the streets is his own familia." Even his buddy Smiley reiterates, "We started the 38th and I'll never forget you, carnal. But I got to think about my family" (91). They all repeat the importance of the family bond. As if to reassure Henry's recognition of such unavoidable obligation, the playwright soon throws in a conflict when white police intend to nab Joey, one of Henry's men, for "stealing" George's car. The enraged Henry (El Pachuco) immediately wants to fight the white regime by challenging the racist police. It is his parents who try to hold him back, symbolizing the surging of the family bond and the duty identity to check him. The mother says, "Henry. No!" and the father stands up before Henry when the latter is about to dash out. When the father shouts, "You will stay here," Henry reacts as the old impetuous Henry:

> HENRY: Get out of my way! (ENRIQUE *powerfully pushes him back and throws* HENRY *to the floor and holds.*)
> ENRIQUE: TE DIGO QUE NO! (*Silent moment,* HENRY *stands up and offers to strike* ENRIQUE. *But something stops him. The realization that if* HE *strikes back or even if* HE *walks out the door, the family bond is irreparably broken.* HENRY *tenses for a moment, then relaxes and embraces his father.* DELLA *goes to them and joins the embrace. Then* DOLORES, *then* LUPE, *then* RUDY. *All embrace in a tight little group.*) (94)

In addition to the newly acquired spirit of self-control inside him, the obligation of family cools Henry's impetuosity and rash reaction. He decides to assume his family responsibility after the long absence from home, not to have any face-to-face conflict with the racist police, and to allow his white allies (George) to take care of the police trouble. At the end of the play, Henry finally learns to be a Chicano taking care of his family and his 38th Street Gang in a smarter way.

IV. The Coalition

Examining Luis Valdez and Amiri Baraka in *Taking It to the Streets*, Harry J. Elam analyzes the narrow perspective of the essentialism and nationalism in the ethnic power movements in the 1960s and 1970s. He finds that "recognizing the limitations of earlier conceptions of black and Chicano identity, contemporary black and Chicano theorists have lobbied for coalitional politics that push beyond the earlier platforms of identity to realize contradictions within subject position and embrace difference" (Elam, *Taking* 8). A farsighted playwright, Valdez has also implanted such a cross-racial coalition in *Zoot Suit*, through the characters of white lawyer George Shearer and socialist activist Alice Bloomfield. As mentioned before, Henry first distrusts his white lawyer's good intentions, but George's persuasive words to explain his genuine willingness to help and to expel Henry's detrimental narrow mindset (only Chicanos are Chicanos' good friends) eventually disarm Henry and induce his trust, a step significant to the collaboration of all the marginalized. Although George does not win the case for Henry, it is very important for us to see that Henry later not only allows George to represent them but also relies on him completely.

Due to her own identity and experience as a Jewish woman, Alice further proves to Henry that no one should be deprived of their basic human rights. She teaches Henry to never give up and she also teaches him to have a united front to fight and to fight against injustice. When Henry repeatedly asks her to speculate on what will happen if their appeal fails (implying his distrust in justice), she explains in Act Two Scene Seven about her conviction.

> [...] I won't have you treat me this way. I never have been able to accept one person pushing another around... pushing me around! Can't you see that's why I'm here? Because I can't stand it

happening to you. Because I'm a Jew, goddammit! I have been there...I have been there! If you lose, I lose. (84)

The simple message Valdez wants to pass through the Jewish activist Alice is that no one person, no one ethnic group, should be discriminated against, which I think is the most important message of Valdez's to his white audience. Because Alice is one of the oppressed, she knows how one feels when one is unjustly treated. Alice is the one who fights back with a conviction that all the oppressed groups should cooperate with each other and this support activity also further confirms her belief because, as Alice tells Henry, they have great support from all kinds of people including "Unions, Mexicans, Negroes, Oakies," and, as she comments, "It's fantastic" (83). This message of minority coalition through Alice is new to the Chicano/a community and to most of the audience.[51] However, Henry does learn to take a chance to try this new way.

Perhaps an unusual reflection of the cross-racial collaboration of the 1970s, the sincere help of the white lawyer and the avid assistance of the Jewish activist display a new way for Chicano Americans to follow in future; i.e., Hispanic groups should not only work together, but also cooperate with whoever is willing to help, and particularly, other marginalized groups. As Laclau and Mouffe state, in addition to constructing systems of equivalence, the underprivileged should work together "though systems of alliances with other forces" (141). Only the

---

[51] Many critics criticize Valdez's sell-out attitude in including a white woman to gratify and satisfy the white (Jewish) theatre-goers (Broyles-Gonzalez 201-03). They criticize Valdez's distortion of history and the arrangements of this fictitious female character and the made-up episode between Alice and Henry. Valdez defends himself by saying that that was not his intention and according to his research there was really such a lady who also developed some relationship with Henry during his imprisonment (Hamilton 280). However, in his later film version of the same work, Valdez downplays the importance of such a female figure and her contribution so as not to lead the audience astray. I think we should move away from the authenticity question and step forward to read the clear message: the oppressed should stand up for each other. For a defense against the bothersome or alienating effect of such an arrangement of the added character Alice, see Hamilton's "Criticism."

Reynas getting together is not enough; only the 38th Street Gang, the Chicano community, and the Hispanic getting united is not enough. They should cooperate with people of different races, genders, and backgrounds because the marginalized share the same history of subjugation. Working together with marginalized groups who have much more in common, they will make a difference.

V. Conclusion

Rewriting history is difficult. Rewriting history of racial trauma and victimization with a purpose to endow one with a new identity is even more difficult. However, Luis Valdez's strategies prove to be effective in arousing Chicanos/as' reflection on and reaction against the hegemony of whites. Like Foucault's concept of genealogy and counter-memory, which distrusts "continuity" in traditional history (Foucault 154), Valdez's rewriting of this particular history of these Chicano/as disrupts canonical American history. Although he departs a little from the historical trajectory and creates his own interpretation of why Hispanic American subjectivity is distorted, he brings forth a new perspective for Chicanos/as to look at themselves closely. Chicanos/as should not accept the passive identity and the pessimistic outlook of life as were given by whites because this version from whites not only distorts their true identity but also gives them internal colonialism. Instead, they should, like Henry Reyna, learn to have a new identity of indigenousness, action, and duty and be prepared to form a coalition with other support or marginal groups so as to strive for the best. Forty years after the Sleepy Lagoon Murder Case and the Zoot Suit Riots, some people still treat the pachuco as base animals, many more still have a distorted identity fixed for the Chicanos/as, and society is still replete with panoptic surveillance and normalizing values for the marginalized. But Valdez knows the time is different; only a new identity—indigenous, active, and dutiful—can allow Chicanos/as to survive better in modern times of radical changes and challenges, so that they too can have their fair share of realizing their American dream.

Chapter 5
Conclusion

With vast land and rich resources, with less historical burden but more liberal minds, America is a country of abundant blessings. It is no wonder for the past four hundred years people from Great Britain and all over the world have swarmed to the country, seeking to realize their American dream. Like the good land attracting people to it with a promising prospect in Eugene O'Neill's *Desire under the Elms*, this blessed land has truly the charm to attract whites and non-whites to strive for the best in it. The American Revolution itself, being the best embodiment of the American dream, has also taught the people everything is possible in this dream land.

Hence, when whites have established this country and have claimed liberty and equality the founding spirits of the dream country, it is very difficult to understand why they have made it so difficult for non-whites to also realize their dreams in this same country. While whites had their dream set on riches and fame, ethnic minorities in the country were still fighting for their basic human rights and dignity. This is the major difference between whites' and non-whites' American dreams.

When Martin Luther King Jr. said, "I have a dream...," he had the painful suffering of his fellow African Americans in his mind. His dream is not to have material success but to have very basic human rights that were only prescribed to whites. August Wilson has a big mind like King's and he'd like to share the same vision with his fellow African Americans in all of his plays. This conviction for African Americans to target their dreams on the spiritual pursuit—the self recognition and equal rights—is clearly conveyed in *The Piano Lesson*. Instead of creating a perfect but impossible hero, Wilson presents his message through a young man full of whites' American dream, Boy Willie, so the audience gets to know chasing material success blindly by even sacrificing African American heritage and pride cannot lead to true success. Furthermore, Wilson also endorses Boy Willie's celebratory attitude to treat African American's afflicted past. People like Berniece, Doaker, and many other Africans either feel ashamed of their past or prefer not to uncover their wounded past. Little do they know such a gloomy view is mainly perpetuated by whites' hegemonic ideology of subjugation. If blacks all demonstrate their courage not to be afraid of death, they will no longer be in the power of whites anymore. Furthermore, instead of feeling inferior to whites, instead of being dominated by white ideology, blacks should really embrace their past and feel proud of their achievement because their labor contributed to help build this beautiful country today. August Wilson believes blacks are beautiful and powerful people and indeed they are. To have a correct understanding of their essence and value, blacks have to write/right their own past. A more important message implied in the play is that they have to cooperate to heal their wounds and to work together to exorcise the distorted past. If they simply follow whites' steps to pursue material success without acknowledging who exactly they are and what enlightenment they can offer to whites, they will not win their ultimate respect and true success.

Frank Chin must have witnessed blacks like August Wilson and people depicted in his plays who are active about fighting to realize their dreams. Although Chinese used to harbor some racial discrimination against blacks, Chin has found an admirable combative spirit from blacks, which is just the right emulation for redressing the emasculated mindset of many Asian men. He has an elevated position for blacks in his *The Chickencoop Chinaman*; Tam Lam and BlackJap Kenji idolize the black boxer, and it is also through a black mentor that Tam's misconceived American dream is disillusioned. After being taught not to escape but to look straight into Chinese Americans through an unbiased and undistorted lens, Tam walks out of the shadow of self-denigration. Moreover, just as Wilson's embracing attitude towards African Americans' past, Chin also sees the contribution of early Chinese immigrants. Through the image of the Iron Moonhunter, Chin connects Chinese railroad workers' labor with the prosperity of the American West. This particular history, implicating a positive past and true value of Chinese Americans, is indispensable for Chinese Americans to envision themselves. The American dream, which awaits Chinese Americans ahead, cannot be achieved without their overcoming their own sense of inferiority, without truly embracing their own past history of humiliation.

Like August Wilson and Frank Chin, Luis Valdez wants to expose how white institutions construct and distort Chicanos/as in *Zoot Suit*. Therefore, if Chicanos/as intend to take this country as their home and further pursue their dreams, they need to get rid of the lens whites use to see them through. Valdez clearly shows how white hegemonic law enforcers and media condemn zoot suitors. But Valdez has his protagonist depart from the original historical figure so that his audience can see that in order to have a beautiful life in America, they must strive to live up to be indigenously unique, active and be men of strong family bonds. Without their own respect for themselves, without their incessant effort to exert themselves, they will not win respect from others.

Influenced by other Civil Rights Movement activists, Valdez also sees the importance of coalition across race boundaries. While Wilson stresses intraracial cooperation, and while Chin presses for the coalition of minority groups, Valdez adds more forces to the united frontline in *Zoot Suit*. He makes white lawyer George Shearer question Henry Reyna, "What difference does it make if I were or were not Chicano?" and though he loses the case, this white lawyer does a good job in defending his Chicano clients. Valdez also includes a female Jewish activist to fight with the Chicanos/as against white oppressors. In an age of globalization, such a united frontline consisting of the mainstream white supporters, the marginalized, the other gender and the other ethnicities truly represents the force of the marginalized and the oppressed.

In a nutshell, the two major common features August Wilson, Frank Chin, and Luis Valdez share are to pursue the spiritual American dream before chasing material success, and to recognize the importance of collective strength in fighting against oppression and in realizing their dreams. Indeed, many ethnic playwrights deal with the imminent issue of dismantling racial subjugation and reconstructing their own history and identity. For example, Lorraine Hansberry's *A Raisin in the Sun* (1959), Amiri Baraka's *The Dutchman* (1964), David Henry Hwang's *The Dance of the Railway* (1982), Philip Gotenda's *Yankee Dawg You Die* (1991), Sherri Moraga's *Giving up the Ghost* (1994), and Silvia Gonzalez S.'s *The Migrant Farmerworker's Son* (1994) address the victimization of non-whites in a white dominated society. Most of these plays focus on the cause and effect of such unjust treatment of minority people. Thus it is really very unique for Wilson, Chin, and Valdez to see the same enlightening point—coalition. Because of their similar history of painful subjugation, these minority groups can make the best of the common ground and know that they should share their reconstructing strategies and power so that their potential and mutual help can be carried out to the fullest extent when they are in the same boat fighting for their due respect and rights.

When discussing ethnic dramas in *A Critical Introduction to Twentieth-Century American Drama*, Bigsby contends, "each racial group in turn has established its own theatres and created its own drama in part, at least, as a means to escape the reductive images offered over the years by a society which invited the world's poor and needy and then consigned them to the periphery of social and cultural life" (373). Bigsby continues to point out the essence of the "minority" theatre is that it acknowledges the multi-ethnic nature of American society; moreover, the multicultural theatre not only expands the subject matter and range of American drama but also "potentially move[s] drama closer to the centre of the lives of those for whom it had seemed both an irrelevance and, at times, an affront" (374). Because these new ethnic theatres have created new myths, deployed their own styles and forged their own values, suddenly these ethnic theatres are "at the centre of dramatic if not political attention" (Bigsby, *Critical Introduction* 374). Hence, American ethnic drama not only had diversified and enriched American drama, but it has also offered the people an invaluable enlightenment and what true tolerance and respect are in a multiethnic society.

Thanks to the efforts of people like August Wilson, Frank Chin, and Luis Valdez, people have learned to know that African Americans, Chinese Americans, and Chicano Americans are worthy of respect. Through their plays like *The Piano Lesson*, *The Chickencoop Chinaman*, and *Zoot Suit*, African Americans, Chinese Americans, and Chicano Americans, and many other people of various ethnic backgrounds should learn that, living in such a country with promises of realization of the American dream, they should not merely pursue the white version of the American dream because material success cannot guarantee a real and decent living, or mutual recognition and respect from their white counterparts. They should look into themselves, deconstruct the distortion constructed by whites in the past, understand their past as conducive to the making of this superpower country on earth, they should appreciate what their forebears have done, and they should also embrace themselves for who they are. Last but not least, they must learn to fight back together the oppression, victimization, and distortion with their own people, with people of other minority groups who have suffered the same subjugation, with people who support true equality. In this way, they will have an equal footage to also realize their own American dreams.

Bibliography

Abbotson, Susan C. W. "What Does August Wilson Teach in The Piano Lesson?: The Place of the Past and Why Boy Willie Knows More Than Berniece." *Journal of American Drama and Theatre* 12.1(2000): 83-101.

Alford, Holly. "The Zoot Suit: Its History and Influence." *Fashion Theory: The Journal of Dress, Body & Culture* 8:2 (Jun 2004): 225-236.

Althusser, Louis. *Lenin and Philosophy and Other Essays*. trans. Ben Brewster. New York, Monthly Review P, 1971.

Ambush, Benny Sato. "Culture Wars." *African American Review* 31.4 (1997): 579-86.

Anderson, Addell Austin. "August Wilson: Overview." *Contemporary Dramatists, 5th ed.* Ed. K. A. Berney, St. James Press, 1993. 6 pars. 29 November 2006 < http://galenet.galegroup.com/>

Andrews, James R. "If God Prosper Us: Daniel Webster and the Historical Foundations of American Nationalism." *Argumentation and Values: Proceedings of the Ninth SCA/AFA Conference on Argumentation*. Ed. Sally Jackson. Annandale, VA: Speech Communication Association, 1995. 21-32.

Arteaga, Alfred. *Chicano Poetics: Heterotexts and Hybridities*. Cambridge: Cambridge U P, 1997.

"August Wilson." *Contemporary Authors Online*, Thomson Gale, 2006. 29 November 2006 < http://galenet.galegroup.com/>

"August Wilson." *Contemporary Literary Criticism*. 29 November 2006 < http://galenet.galegroup.com/>

Babcock, Granger. "Looking for a Third Space: El Pachuco and Chicano Nationalism in Luis Valdez's *Zoot Suit*." *Staging Difference: Cultural Pluralism in American Theatre and Drama*. Ed. Marc Maufort, Peter Lang. 1995. 215-25.

Banks, James A. *Teaching Strategies for Ethnic Studies*. Fourth Edition. Boston: Allyn and Bacon, Inc, 1987.

Bhabha, Homi. *The Location of Culture*. New York: Routledge, 1994.

Biedler, Philip D. "'King August': August Wilson in His Time." *Michigan Quarterly Review* 45.4(2006):575-97.

Bigsby, C. W. E. *A Critical Introduction to Twentieth-Century American Drama 3: Beyond Broadway*. Cambridge: Cambridge UP, 1985.

---. *Modern American Drama, 1945-1990*. Cambridge: Cambridge UP, 1992.

Bissiri, Amadou. "Aspects of Africanness in August Wilson's Drama: Reading

The Piano Lesson through Wole Soyinka's Drama." *African American Review* 30.1 (1996): 99-113.Boan, Devon. "Call-and-response: Parallel "Slave Narrative" in August Wilson's *The Piano Lesson*." *African American Review* 32.2 (1998): 263-272.

Broyles-González, Yolanda. "The New Professionalism: *Zoot Suit* in the Mainstream." *El Teatro Campesino: Theater in the Chicano Movement.* U of Texas P, 1994. 177-205.

Brustein, Robert. "The Lesson of *The Piano Lesson*." *The New Republic* 202.21 (1990): 28-30.

Campbell, Jane. *Mythic Black Fiction: The Transformation of History.* Knoxville: U of Tennessee P, 1986.

Cernkovich, Stephen A. et al. "Race, Crime, and the American Dream." *Journal of Research in Crime & Delinquency* 37.2(2000): 131-68.

Chan, Sucheng. *Asian Americans: An Interpretive History.* Boston: Twayne, 1991.

-----. "Introduction." *Entry Denied: Exclusion and the Chinese Community in America, 1882-1943.* ed. Sucheng Chan. Philadelphia: Temple UP, 1991. Vii-xv.

Cheung, King-Kok. "The Woman Warrior versus the Chinaman Pacific: Must a Chinese American Critic Choose between Feminism and Heroism?" *Conflicts in Feminism.* ed. Marianne Hirsch and Evelyn Fox Keller. New York: Routledge, 1990. 234-51.

Chin, Frank. *The Chickencoop Chinaman and The Year of the Dragon.* Seattle and London: U of Washington P, 1981.

---, Jeffery Paul Chan, Lawson Fusao Inado, and Shawn Wong, eds. *Aiiieeeee!: An Anthology of Asian-American Writers.* Washington D.C.: Howard UP, 1974, 1983.

Chin, Frank and Jeffery Paul Chan, "Racist Love." *Seeing Through Shuck.* Ed. Rochard Kostelanez. New York: Ballantine, 1972.

Ching, Mei-Ling. "Wrestling against History." *Theater* 19.3 (1988 Summer-Fall): 70-71.

Chu, Patricia P. "*Tripmaster Monkey*, Frank Chin, and the Chinese Heroic Tradition." *Arizona Quarterly* 53.3(1997): 117-39.

Chua, Cheng Lok. "*The Year of the Dragon* by Frank Chin." *A Resource Guide to Asian American Literature.* Ed. Cynthia Wong, Sau-ling and Stephen H. Sumida. New York: Modern Language Association of American, 2001. 175-84.

Danico, Mary Yu and Franklin Ng. *Asian American Issues.* Westport, Connecticut: Greenwood P, 2004.

Davis, R. G. and Betty Diamond. "*Zoot Suit*: From the Barrio to Broadway." *Ideologies & Literature* 3:15. January-March 1981. 124-33. 24 April 2006 < http://galenet.galegroup.com >

Davy, Daniel. "The Enigmatic God: Mask and Myth in *Zoot Suit*." *Journal of American Drama and Theatre* 15:1 (2003 Winter). 71-87.

DeSantis, Alan D. "Selling the American Dream myth to black southerners: The

Chicago Defender and the great migration of 1915-1919." *Western Journal of Communication* 62.4(1998): 474-511.

De Vries, Hilary. "A Song in Search of Itself." *American Theatre* 3.10(1987): 22-5.

Eder, Richard. "Theater: '*Zoot Suit*,' Chicano Music-Drama." *The New York Times* March 26, 1979, p. c-13. 24 April 2006 <http://galenet.galegroup.com >

Elam, Harry J. Jr. *The Past as Present in the Drama of August Wilson*. Ann Arbor: U of Michigan P, 2004.

---. *Taking It to the Streets: The Social Progest Theater of Luis Valdez and Amiri Baraka*. Ann Arbor: U of Michigan P, 2001

---. "The Dialectics of August Wilson's *The Piano Lesson*." *Theatre Journal*. 52.3 (2000): 361-79.

Elkins, Marilyn Roberson. *August Wilson: A Casebook*. New York: Garland, 1994.

Fanon, Franz. *Black Skin, White Masks*. New York: Grove, 1967.

Fisher, Walter R. "Reaffirmation and Subversion of the American Dream." *Quarterly Journal of Speech* 59 (1973): 160-67.

Fitzgerald, F. Scott. *The Great Gatsby*. New York: Cambridge U, 1991.

Fong, Timothy P. "The History of Asians in America." *Asian Americans: Experiences and Perspectives*. Ed. Timothy P. Fong and Larry H. Shinagawa. Upper Saddle River, New Jersey: Prentice Hall, 2000. 13-30.

---. *The Contemporary Asian American Experience: Beyong dhte Model Minority*. Upper Saddle River, New Jersey: Prentice Hall, 1998.

Foucault, Michel. *Language, Counter-memory, Practice: Selected Essays and Interviews*. Ed. Donald F. Bouchard. Trans. Donald F. Bouchard and Sherry Simon. Ithaca, New York: Cornell UP, 1977.

---. *Discipline and Punish: The Birth of the Prison*. Trans. Alan Sheridan. New York: Vintage Books, 1995.

Galons, David and Lynn Spampinato, ed. *Zoot Suit*. *Drama for Students: Presenting Analysis, Context and Criticism on Commonly Studied Drama*. Vol. 5. Detroit, Michigan: Gale Research, 1988. 268-86.

Gelb, Hal. "Theater". *Nation* 274:22. 6/10/2002. 35-36.

Glover, Margaret E. "Two Notes on August Wilson: The Songs of a Marked Man." *Theater* 19.3 (1988 Summer-Fall): 69-70.

Goshert, John Charles. "Frank Chin." *Asian American Writers*. Ed. Deborah L. Madsen. Detroit, MI: Gale, 2005. 44-57.

Graham-White, Anthony. "Frank Chin: Overview" *Contemporary Dramatists*. 5th ed., Ed. K. A. Berney. St. James Press, 1993. <http://galenet.galegroup.com>

Gutierez-Jones, Carl. "Legal Rhetoric and Cultural Critique: Notes toward Guerrilla Writing." *Diacritics: A Review of Contemporary Criticism* 20:4 (1990 Winter): 57-73.

Gutman, Amy. *Multiculturalism: Examining the Politics of Recognition*. Princeton: Princeton UP, 1994.

Habermas, Jurgen. "Struggles for Recognition in the Democratic Constitutional

State." *Multiculturalism: Examining the Politics of Recognition.* Ed. Gutmann. Princeton: Princeton UP, 1994. 107-48.

Hall, Stuart. "The Question of Cultural Identity." *Modernity and Its Futures.* Cambridge: Polity Press in Association with the Open University, 1992. 273-326.

Hamilton, Carole. "Criticism." *"Zoot Suit." Drama for Students.* Vol. 5. Detroit, Michigan: Gale Research, 1998. 268-86.

Harris, Trudier. "August Wilson's Folk Traditions." *Modern Dramatists: A Casebook of Major British, Irish, and American Playwrights.* Ed. Kimball King. NY: Routledge, 2001. 369-82.

Hayes, Corlis. *A Critical and Historical Analysis of Five Major Plays by August Wilson.* Diss. Southern Illinois UP, 1993.

Heyen, William. "Arthur Miller's *Death of Salesman* and the American Dream." *Modern Critical Interpretations of Arthur Miller's Death of a Salesman.* ed. Harold Bloom. New York: Chelsea House, 1988. 47-58.

"Hispanic." 24 April 2006 <http://en.wikipedia.org/wiki/Hispanic >

Hochschild, Jennifer L. *Facing up to the American Dream: Race, Class, and the Soul of the Nation.* Princeton, New Jersey: Princeton UP, 1995.

Huerta, Jorge A. "Chicano Theater: Themes and Forms." *Chicano Theater: Themes and Forms.* Bilingual Press/Editorial Bilingüe. 1982. 274 p.

---. "Luis Valdez: Overview." *Contemporary Dramatists.* 5th ed., Ed. K. A. Berney. St. James Press, 1993. 24 April 2006 < http://galenet.galegroup.com >

---. *Chicano Drama: Performance, Society and Myth.* Cambridge: Cambridge UP, 2000.

---. "*Zoot Suit* and Other Plays." An Introduction to *Zoot Suit* and Other Plays. Arte Publico Press. 1992. 7-20. 24 April 2006 < http://galenet.galegroup.com >

Hume, Kathryn. *American Dream, American Nightmare: Fiction Since 1960.* Urbana and Chicago: University of Illinois Press, 2002.

Jacobs, Elizabeth. *Mexican American Literature: the Politics of Identity.* London; New York: Routledge, 2006.

Jimenez, Francisco. "Dramatic Principles of the Teatro Campesino." *The Identification and Analysis of Chicano Literature.* Ed. Francisco Jimenez. New York: Bilingual P, 1979. 117-32.

Kanellos, Nicolas. *Luis Miguel Valdez. Dictionary of Literary Biography,* Volume 122: Chicano Writers, Second Series. A Bruccoli Clark Layman Book. Ed. Francisco A. Lomeli, and Carl R. Shirley. U of South Carolina. The Gale Group, 1992. 281-292. 24 April 2006 < http://galenet.galegroup.com >.

Kim, Daniel Y. *Writing Manhood in Black and Yellow: Ralph Ellison, Frank Chin, and the Literary Politics of Identity.* Stanford: Stanford UP, 2005.

Kim, Elaine. *Asian American Literature: An Introduction to the Writing and Their Social Content.* Philadelphia: Temple UP, 1982.

Laclau, Ernesto and Chantal Mouffe. *Hegemony & Socialist Strategy: Towards a*

Radical Democratic Politics. London: Verso, 1985.

Lawrence, Keith and John Dye. "Frank Chin." *Dictionary of Literary Biography, Volume 206: Twentieth-Century American Western Writers, First Series*. A Bruccoli Clark Layman Book. Ed. Richard H. Cracroft. Gale Group, 1999. 42-50. 31 pars. 16 July 2007 < http://galenet.galegroup.com >.

Lee, David Leiwei. *Imagining the Nation: Asian American Literature and Cultural Consent*. Stanford: Stanford UP, 1998.

---. "The Formation of Frank Chin and Formation of Chinese American Literature." *Asian Americans: Comparative and Global Perspectives*. Ed. Shirley Hune and Hyung-chan Kim. Pullman: Washington State UP, 1991. 211-23.

Lee, Josephine. *Performing Asian America: Race and Ethnicity on the Contemporary Stage*. Philadelphia: Temple UP, 1997.

Lee, Robert G. *Orientals: Asian Americans in Popular Culture*. Philadelphia: Temple UP, 1999.

Lee, Yu-cheng. "The Politics of Remembering in Donald Duk." *Cultural Identity and Chinese American Literature*. Ed. Te-hsing Shan and Wen-ching Ho. Taipei: Academia Sinica, 1994.

Lim, Shirley Geok-lin. "'Growing with Stories'": Chinese American Identities, Textual Identities." *Teaching American Ethnic Literatures*. Albuquerque: U of New Mexico P, 1996. 273-97.

---. "The Ambivalent American: Asian American Literature on the Cusp." *Reading the Literatures of Asian America*. Philadelphia: Temple Up, 1992. 13-32.

Little, Jonathan. "August Wilson." Dictionary of Literary Biography, Volume 228: Twentieth-Century American Dramatists, Second Series. A Bruccoli Clark Layman Book. Ed. Christopher J. Wheatley. The Catholic University of America. Gale Group, 2000. 289-302. 55 pars. Literature Resource Center. 3 December 2007 < http://galenet.galegroup.com >.

Lloyd, David. "Race under Representation." *Oxford Literary Review* 13.1-2 (1991):62-94.

Louie, Steve and Glenn Omastsu. Eds. *Asian Americans: The Movement and the Moment*. Los Angeles: UCLA Asian American Studies Center P, 2001.

Luis (Miguel) Valdez". *Contemporary Authors Online*. The Gale Group, 2001. 24 April 2006 < http://galenet.galegroup.com >

Lyman, Stanford M. *Chinese Americans*. New York: Random House, 1974.

Madden, David. ed. *American Dreams, American Nightmares*. Carbondale and Edwardsville: Southern Illinois UP, 1970.

Maeda, Daryl J. "Black Panthers, Red Guards, and Chinamen: Constructing Asian American Identity though Performing Blackness, 1969-1972. *American Quarterly* 57.4 (Dec 2005): 1079-1103.

Mark, Diane Mei Lin and Genger Chih. *A Place Called Chinese American*. USA: Organization of Chinese Americans, Inc., 1982.

Martinez, Julio A. and Francisco A. Lomeli. Ed. *Chicano Literature: A Reference*

Guide. Westport, Connecticut: Greenwood P, 1985.

Mazon, Mauricio. *The Zoot-Suit Riots: The Psychology of Symbolic Annihilation*. Austin, Texas: U of Texas P, 1984.

McClain, Charles J. *In Search of Equality: The Chinese Struggle against Discrimination in Nineteenth-Century American*. Berkeley: U of California P, 1994.

McDonald, Dorothy Ritsuko. "Introduction." *The Chickencoop Chinaman and The Year of the Dragon*. Seattle: U of Washington P, 1981, ix-xxix.

McWilliams, Carey. *North from Mexico: The Spanish-Speaking People of the United States*. Philadelphia: J. B. Lippincott, 1949.

Memmi, Albert. *The Colonizer and the Colonized*. Trans Howard Greenfeld. Exp. Ed. 1965. Boston: Beacon, 1991.

Miller, Arthur. *Death of a Salesman*. *The Heath Introduction to Drama*. 3rd edition. Ed. Jordan Y. Miller. Lexington, Massachusetts: D. C. Heath and Company, 1988. 871-954.

Min, Pyong Gap. "Major Issues Related to Asian American Experiences." *Asian Americans: Contemporary Trends and Issues*. Ed. Pyong Gap Min. Thousand Oaks, California: Pine Forge P, 2006. 80-107.

Mogen, David, Mark Busby, and Paul Bryant. *The Frontier Experience and the American Dream*. College Station: Texas A & M UP, 1989.

Morales, Armando and Ando Sangrando. *I Am Bleeding: A Study of Mexican American-Police Conflict*. La Puente, California: Perspectiva, 1974.

Morales, Michael. "Ghosts on the Piano: August Wilson and the Representation of Black American History." *May All Your Fences Have Gates: Essays on the Drama of August Wilson*. Ed. Alan Nadel. Iowa City: U of Iowa P, 1994. 105-15.

Nguyen, Viet Thanh. "The Remasculinization of Chinese America: Race, Violence, and the Novel." *American Literary History* 12.1-2(2000): 130-57.

Nadel, Alan. Ed. *May All Your Fences Have Gates: Essays on the Drama of August Wilson*. Iowa City: U of Iowa P, 1994.

Novick, Julius. "No Cheers for the 'Chinaman'." *The New York Times*, 18 June 1972 Section 2, p. 3. Reproduced in *Literature Resource Center*. <http://galenet.galegroup.com>

Oregon Shakespeare Festival: 2006 Souvenir Program. Ashland, Oregon: Oregon Shakespeare Festival, 2006.

Paredes, Raymund A. "The Evolution of Chicano Literature." *Three American Literatures: Essays in Chicano, Native American, and Asian-American Literature of Teachers of American Literature*. New York: Modern Language Association of America, 1982. 33-79.

Pereira, Kim. *August Wilson and the African-American Odyssey*. U of Illinois P, 1995.

---. "August Wilson: Overview." *Reference Guide to American Literature, 3rd ed.*, Ed. Jim Kamp. St. James Press, 1994.

Plum, Jay. "Blues, History, and the Dramaturgy of August Wilson." *African*

American Review 27. 4(1993): 561–7.

Ramirez, Catherine S. "Saying 'Nothing'." *Frontiers* 27.3(2006): 1-35.

Ramirez, Elizabeth. "Chicano Theatre Reaches the Professional Stage: Luis Valdez's *Zoot Suit*." *Teaching American Ethnic Literatures: Nineteen Essays*. Ed. John R. Albuquerque: U of New Mexico P, 1996. 193-207.

Rothstein, Mervyn. "Round Five for a Theatrical Heavyweight." *New York Times* 15 Apr. 1990, sec2:3.

Said, Edward. *Culture and Imperialism*. New York: Alfred A. Knopf, 1993.

---. *Orientalism*. New York: Vintage Books, 1979.

Savran, David. "An interview with Luis Valdez." *In Their Own Words: Contemporary American Playwrights*. Theatre Communications Group. 1988. 257-71.

---. "An Interview with August Wilson." *In Their Own Words*. New York: Theatre Communications Group, 1988. 288-305.

Scanlan, Tom. *Family, Drama, American Dreams*. Westport, Connecticut: Green Wood P, 1978.

Sevareid, Eric. "The American Dream." *The American Dream in Literature*. ed. Stanley A. Werner, Jr. New York: Charles Scribner's Sons, 1970.

Shafer, Yvonne. "Breaking Barriers: August Wilson." *Staging Difference: Cultural Pluralism in American Theatre and Drama*. Ed. Marc Maufort and Peter Lang, 1995. 267-85.

Shan, Te-hsing. *Inscriptions and Representations: Chinese American Literary and Cultural Studies*. Taipei: Rye Field, 2000.

---. and Wen-ching Ho. *Cultural Identity and Chinese American Literature*. Taipei: Academia Sinica, 1994.

Shannon, Sandra G. *The Dramatic Vision of August Wilson*. Washington, D. C. Howard UP, 1995.

---. "The Ground on Which I Stand: August Wilson's Perspective on African American Women." *May All Your Fences Have Gates: Essays on the Drama of August Wilson*. Ed. Alan Nadel. Iowa: University of Iowa Press, 1994. 150-64.

---. "The Good Christian's Come and Gone: The Shifting Role of Christianity in August Wilson Plays." *Melus* 16(1989-90): 127–42.

Shimakawa, Karen. *National Abjection: The Asian American Body Onstage*. Durham, N.C.: Duke UP, 2002.

Shirley, Carl R. and Paula W. Shirley. *Understanding Chicano Literature*. Columbia, South Carolina: U of South Carolina P, 1988.

Takaki, Ronald. *Strangers from a Different Shore*. Boston: Little Brown, 1989.

Taylor, Charles. "The Politics of Recognition." *Multiculturalism: Examining the Politics of Recognition*. Ed. Gutman, 25-74.

Torfing, Jacob. *New Theories of Discourse: Laclau, Mouffe and Zizek*. New York: Blackwell, 1999.

"2004 American Community Survey Data Profile Highlights." 24 April 2006 < http://factfinder.census.gov/servlet>

Valdez, Luis. *Zoot Suit and Other Plays*. Houston: Art Publico Press, 1992.

Wand, David Hsin-Fu. "The Chinese-American Literary Scene: A Galaxy of Poets and Lone Playwright." *Proceedings of the Comparative Literature Symposium*, vol. IX, 1978, pp. 121-46. Reprinted in *Drama Criticism*. Vol.7. Reproduced in *Literature Resource Center*. http://galenet.galegroup.com

Wang, Hsiu-hui. *Racial Discrimination and Gender: The Experiences of Chinese American Men before WWII*. Taipei: Yunchen, 2006.

Wattenberg, Richard. " From 'Horse Opera' History to Hall of Mirrors: Luis Vialdez's Bandidi! Modern Drama 41.3(1998): 411-22. ProQuest. Online. <http://0-proquest.umi.com.>

Wei, William. *The Asian American Movement*. Philadelphia: Temple UP, 1993.

Wiley, Catherine. "Teatro Chicano and the Seduction of Nostalgia." *Melus* 23.1 (1998): 99-115. *ProQuest*. Online. Internet. <http://0-proquest.umi.com.>

Wilson, August. *Gem of the Ocean*. New York: Theatre Communication Group, 2006.

---. *The Piano Lesson*. New York, Plume, 1990.

---. *Joe Turner's Come and Gone*. New York: Plume, 1988.

---. *Fences*. New York: New American Library, 1987.

Wolfe, Peter. *August Wilson*. New York: Twayne, 1999.

Wong, Morrison G. " Chinese Americans." *Asian Americans: Contemporary Trends and Issues*. 2nd ed. Ed. Pyong Gap Min. Thousand Oaks: Pine Forge P, 2006. 110-45.

Wong, Sau-ling. *Reading Asian American Literature: From Necessity to Extravagance*. Princeton, N. J.: Princeton UP, 1993.

---. "The Yellow and the Black: The African American Presence in Sinophone Chinese American Literature." *Chung Wai Literary Monthly* 34.04 (September 2005): 15-53.

Wong, Shelley Sunn. "Frank Chin: Overview." *Reference Guide to American Literature*. 3rd ed. Ed. Jim Kamp. St. James Press, 1994. Reproduced in *Literature Resource Center*. <http://galenet.galegroup.com>.

Woodyard, George. "Chicano Theatre." *Cambridge Guide to American Theatre*. ed. Don B. Wilmeth and Tice L. Miller. Cambridge: Cambridge U P, 1996.

Index

Tsui-fen Jiang

Dr. Tsui-fen Jiang is a Professor in the English Department at National Chengchi University in Taipei, Taiwan. Dr. Jiang completed her Ph.D. in Comparative Literature at the University of Washington in Seattle, Washington.